GLOBAL MANIFEST DESTINY

GROWING YOUR BUSINESS IN A BORDERLESS ECONOMY

JOHN A. CASLIONE • ANDREW R. THOMAS

Dearborn™
Trade Publishing
A **Kaplan Professional** Company

This publication is designed to provide accurate and authoritative information in regard to the subject matter covered. It is sold with the understanding that the publisher is not engaged in rendering legal, accounting, or other professional service. If legal advice or other expert assistance is required, the services of a competent professional person should be sought.

Senior Acquisitions Editor: Jean Iversen
Senior Managing Editor: Jack Kiburz
Interior Design: Lucy Jenkins
Cover Design: design literate, inc.
Typesetting: the dotted i

Library of Congress Cataloging-in-Publication Data

Caslione, John A.
    Global manifest destiny : growing your business in a borderless economy /
John A. Caslione and Andrew R. Thomas.
        p.   cm.
    Includes bibliographical references and index.
    ISBN 0-7931-4502-3
    1. International business enterprises—Management. 2. Small business—
Management. I. Thomas, Andrew R. II. Title.
    HD62.4 .C369 2002
    658'.049—dc21
                                                              2001003420

Dearborn Trade books are available at special quantity discounts to use for sales promotions, employee premiums, or educational purposes. Please call our Special Sales Department to order or for more information, at 800-621-9621, ext. 4410, or write Dearborn Trade Publishing, 155 N. Wacker Drive, Chicago, IL 60606-1719.

CASLIONE DEDICATION

To my mother and father and to my brother, who were by my side in the very beginning and who are by my side still, after so many years.

THOMAS DEDICATION

To my mom and dad, whose unconditional love and unwavering support have been there always.

CONTENTS

CHAPTER 1

GLOBAL MANIFEST DESTINY

As we travel and speak around the world, business leaders continually query us, "What is a global company?" We find that astute business leaders readily understand the need to take their respective companies to a global position. But surprisingly few know how to get there. Business leaders seem to be searching for something they can't quite put their finger on.

Standing at the dawn of the third millennium, we observe the complete and inevitable economic integration of all humankind, what we call global manifest destiny.

From our perspective, the march of human history has been more influenced by the desire for economic integration than by any other single factor. In fact, the origins of civilization itself are rooted in the notion that we as a species have sought to be connected for the purposes of trade and commerce. In many ways, we as human beings are seeking to re-create the time in our past when we came together in organized societies for the first time.

ECONOMIC INTEGRATION IS INEVITABLE

Economic integration is not a revolutionary idea. Even the most disinterested observer can see that the world's population is becoming more connected and interdependent. It is the inevitable nature of global manifest destiny that makes it compelling and imperious to companies and to the people who lead them.

Just as information technology has become fundamental within the structure of any business, so, too, must the application of global manifest destiny. Even the most backwards-thinking company will admit, however grudgingly, that information technology has become an inescapable reality and one of the most important strategic assets of any organization. Global manifest destiny must be viewed in the same way. To fail to recognize and respond to the inevitable integration of all humankind is to ensure future failure for any human enterprise.

In today's fast-growing world economy, even the companies that refuse to recognize and accept global manifest destiny will have to face competition from abroad. Global competition is everywhere, and if it's not already in your face, it will surely arrive in your neighborhood in the near future.

Companies can no longer barricade the doors, keep the faith, and assume competitors from all over the world will pass over them in the night like the angel of death. Global economic integration is permeating every industry and directly affecting every long-term business plan—without exception. Global manifest destiny has its hands everywhere, and it is here to stay.

This reality mandates that companies and the people who run them look at their entire organization from a global perspective. This recognition must not be mere lip service to what is happening outside the domestic marketplace. Unfortunately, it too often is.

We have each seen the many business leaders who, at one time or another, seem to care about the real global opportunities facing their company, only to lose focus when the next big domestic deal closes. These individuals, at the expense of their company's survival, either knowingly or unwittingly disregard global business in favor of domestic. They justify it by saying such things as "We already have an export office or an international department"; "We already do business in Mexico and Canada"; "This is the way it was done in the past"; or "The last time we tried to go global we got burned in [insert China or any South American country here]."

In most situations, leaders who neglect to honestly evaluate the requirements, risks, and rewards of becoming a global company are taking their companies down a very dangerous road. Such lack of foresight and vision might be labeled gross dereliction of their corporate responsibilities in the face of the realities of the new global economy.

We have encountered such individuals throughout our careers and have concluded that it is extremely difficult, if not impossible, to convince them of global manifest destiny and the realities their companies will face in the future. For some, their only hope may be divine intervention.

MOVING TO A GLOBAL POSITION

On the other hand, those leaders who intuitively sense global manifest destiny are preparing their companies to move from a present domestic-bound position to a truly global one.

Those companies that firmly acknowledge and successfully reply to the mandates of global manifest destiny will be the leaders in their respective industries. Just as those organizations that embraced information technology have become key players within their environments, so, too, will the companies that understand and embrace the precepts of global manifest destiny.

If anything appears to be obvious in our world today, it is that all of this "coming together" is a new and powerful force linking the world in a web of trade and investment. But the earliest historical writings make it clear that humans have always sought economic connections. The new global economy is actually a vision as old as time itself, one that arguably began not with the European age of maritime exploration five centuries ago, but with the Phoenicians, Vikings, Chinese, and other great trading peoples who dreamed of the unification of markets. The new global economy is not a new phenomenon. The expansion around the Nile in 3000 B.C. and the European colonialism of the 18th and 19th centuries were both global manifest destiny in their eras, just as the globalization movement is today.

Terms such as *globalization* and *global economy* are so widely used in current-day lexicon that they are increasingly viewed by many as meaningless or self-evident. Speculators tell us that because of globalization, seemingly stable economies can be brought to their knees almost overnight. Yet, does the use of the word *globalization* justify the actions of self-absorbed individuals and institutions as they almost instantaneously bankrupt 45 million Brazilian farmers? Shareholders and investors use the term *global economy* when they demand that companies turn immediate profits or face retribution from the markets. Does the assertion of the global economy give traders the right to compel a company to forgo its long-term strategy in favor of constantly producing damaging short-term returns? The answer is a resounding and unequivocal "no" to both questions.

Why is it then, at the beginning of the 21st century, that economies and businesses across the world are being held hostage to globalization and the global economy? It's because these terms mean almost everything and nothing at the same time.

WHAT IS GLOBAL MANIFEST DESTINY?

Global manifest destiny, on the other hand, takes the long view of what is happening today and explains it within a historical context. Events that are taking place today are only snapshots of what humans have been trying to accomplish since the beginning of recorded history: total and complete economic integration on a global scale.

Global manifest destiny is compelling businesses to look at themselves in completely new and revolutionary ways. Because of it, markets for goods, services, finance, and information have moved rapidly and tightly across borders. Barriers to the flow of trade and investment have begun to fall, and deregulation is spreading throughout the world as ideological divisions collapse and the cost of communication and data transmission plummet.

Global manifest destiny is providing firms with enormous opportunities to not only sell and invest in previously sheltered markets and form growing global alliances, but also to leverage technological breakthroughs to sell to expanded markets. Companies can access components and technology globally, secure financing by tapping world markets, and obtain human talent from a multitude of nations.

The opportunities appear limitless. Nevertheless, success will not be achieved without tremendous insight and understanding. Only those organizations that truly grasp the magnitude of global manifest destiny and adapt their corporate culture and processes for the long term will achieve greatness in the future.

Our experience tells us that it is entirely possible for a company to properly position itself to take full advantage of the inevitable economic integration of humankind. Those companies that leverage global manifest destiny are the ones that become truly global companies. The firms that recognize, embrace, and assimilate global manifest destiny as part of the very fabric of their organizations will undoubtedly be the leaders in their respective industries and will be best positioned to exploit global business opportunities. Those who don't risk becoming irrelevant within a matter of years.

In reality, very few businesses anywhere in the world have been able to create the culture as well as design and implement the processes needed to achieve a truly worldwide presence for their products and services. Only a few companies profoundly understand what global manifest destiny is really all about.

THE PRESENT-DAY DRIVERS
OF GLOBAL MANIFEST DESTINY

Although global manifest destiny has been with us since the origin of civilization, three drivers are enlarging its current scope: increasing global interdependence, accelerating rate of change, and new information technology.

Increasing Global Interdependence

Like all popular concepts meant to cover a variety of phenomena, *interdependence* has numerous meanings. To better understand interdependence and to make it more useful to our discussion, we must begin by asking what interdependence is, particularly as it relates to global manifest destiny.

Interdependence refers to a condition of interconnectivity and interchange. Interdependence can increase, as it has been doing on most levels since the end of World War II; and it can also decline, as it did, at least in economic terms, during the Great Depression of the 1930s.

Global manifest destiny, on the other hand, implies that economic integration is continuously moving toward a defined end. Thus, for a network of relationships, business or otherwise, to be considered truly global, it must include multicontinental distances, not simply regional networks. Distance is variable, ranging from adjacency (between France and Germany) to opposite sides of the globe (the United States and China). Global manifest destiny is shrinking distance on a large scale.

Now, more than any other time in history, we are experiencing a period of increasing global interdependence in so many aspects of our lives, most notably in our business lives. And as global interdependence continues to accelerate, we must learn its critical dimensions, if for no other reason than to maintain some measure of control over our decisions and actions amid this increasingly fast-moving phenomenon.

One of the great lessons to be learned from the past decade is that while the integration of the world economy increasingly demands a higher level of global interdependence of business, the global economy is not a zero sum game. With each decision, global business leaders set off a sequence of consequences at many levels and over extended periods of time, within their own organizations and in other globally interdependent and inter-connected businesses and organizations.

Accelerating Rate of Change

Entire markets and industries from around the world are changing faster than most business leaders can reinvent and transform their companies. This accelerated rate of change in business is one reason global business will remain in a continu-ous state of transition.

We are confronted with a new era of tremendous change and ambiguity, feeling sometimes as though we are accelerating at the speed of light, possibly even out of control at times. We are eyewitnesses to the first truly interdependent, interconnected, and integrated global economy. The walls between countries, com-panies, and markets around the world continue to fall. People, information, labor, and capital move in and out of these same countries, companies, and markets as never before.

New Information Technology

The last of the key drivers contributing to global manifest destiny is the rapid deployment of new information and communication technology. With such technology, it is commonplace today to export white-collar work around the world. Computer programmers in San Jose and Bangalore will communicate with engineers in Munich and Sydney to help develop products that are manufactured in São Paolo and sold in the United States. Information technology is transforming business at a global level, at speeds unimaginable in the past.

The cost of information technology is dropping faster than the cost of any other previous technology. In the past 30 years, the real price of computer processing power has declined by more than 90,000 percent, an average of 35 percent per year. As a result, this technology has become more affordable to businesses and consumers alike. And with such increased affordability, technology has been adopted and deployed in virtually every aspect of the economy worldwide, providing a competitive advantage to those companies savvy enough to know how to tap into it.

Beyond reducing the costs and accelerating the speed of current traditional operations such as manufacturing and communications, entire new applications and business opportunities for the ongoing release of new technologies are being created. For example, with the new wireless technology, we will soon be able to safely and reliably transfer high-speed, broadband digital communications directly to and from our mobile phones. Moreover, by improving this access directly to businesses and consumers—information on prices and products, for example—information technology enables businesses to make more informed decisions and thus operate more smoothly, and generally utilize, most efficiently, a company's resources or an individual's time globally.

Information technology directly and unmistakably impacts the global economy as it connects all markets, industrialized as well as emerging, for both the production and consumption of products as well as the generation and flow of capital. Global manifest destiny, in turn, incites increased competition and accelerates the transfer of technology throughout the world in the form of enhanced economic integration.

Without a greater appreciation of information technology and a deeper respect for its tremendous power to shape business in the future, many businesses will find it virtually impossible to survive in the new global economy.

The effects of these drivers have brought global manifest destiny to a much more discernible and attainable level for many companies. New economies and efficiencies of scale have been created. Not too long ago, only a few companies had the resources to compete on a global scale. Presently, almost any size firm, with the ambition to do so, can become a global company. The drivers of present-day global manifest destiny have increased this possibility. For companies looking to achieve core global competencies in these and other areas, this book will provide the road map.

GLOBAL MANIFEST DESTINY AND MULTINATIONALS

Some say global manifest destiny is concentrating market power in the hands of a few large corporations. Every day, it seems, we read of new, global megamergers and how those mergers are putting a few big companies in control of our markets and our lives. Nevertheless, General Motors, Ford, and Toyota combined control less of the world's automobile market today than GM alone controlled in 1950. From 1988 to 1998, the top five high-tech companies' shares of worldwide sales in computer hardware, computer software, and long-distance telephony actually declined by 30 percent.

According to the International Chamber of Commerce (ICC), more than 60,000 companies operate outside of their home countries, and more than 35 percent of these firms are from developing countries.

As global companies move into local markets, local companies move into global markets. Even the venerable Tetley Tea Company in the United Kingdom is now owned by a conglomerate from India.

Typically, it is assumed that most firms in industrialized countries, faced with slackening rates of growth and increased foreign competition in their domestic markets, will try to sell their products and services in less developed markets, leveraging their domestic competitive advantage internationally. Later, they will try to consolidate their position in these markets, and, eventually, establish a dominant position worldwide.

The global landscape is, however, no longer the sole domain of multinational behemoths originating from North America, Europe, and Japan. It is now populated by an array of companies, including a growing number of small and medium-size firms from countries all over the world. Domestic market leaders from emerging economies are venturing into international markets as once-protected home markets open up to foreign competition. State monopolies are also becoming privatized and are competing with industrialized nations. In short, global manifest destiny has set the stage for only the fittest to survive—regardless of size.

The logarithmic expansion of the world's economy over the past decade has provided the opportunity for more and more companies to establish a truly global presence for their products and services. Now smaller companies beyond the Fortune 500 or Global 1000 are able to move beyond simple exporting and establish themselves as worldwide companies with a powerful global reach.

Just ten years ago, the chance to become a major player on the world stage was reserved almost exclusively for the richest and most powerful companies in any given industry. Conducting global business outside of mere exporting was simply too costly and time-consuming for most companies. The past decade, however, has witnessed a transformation in the basic requirements needed to establish a global firm.

GLOBAL MANIFEST DESTINY
AND THE REST OF US

In many ways, the big guys opened the door for everybody else. Huge, multinational conglomerates made the necessary investments in infrastructure or forced local governments to do so on their behalf. Across the world, telecommunication systems have been dramatically upgraded. Transportation networks have become more efficient. Trade barriers have been relaxed considerably. As a result, the door is open for smaller companies to get their share of the ever-expanding world economy.

Nevertheless, in far too many cases, senior management, employees, stakeholders, and, even more dishearteningly, Wall Street mistakenly label a smaller firm as a *global company* if it exports its products or service. There is nothing inherently wrong with exporting. For some companies, exporting works quite well—especially for those firms whose products or services are universally accepted throughout the world's major markets.

Nike Air Jordans, Cartier Watches, and Sony Walkmans are pretty much used the same way all over the world. Whether in Chicago, Copenhagen, Cairo, or Cleveland, people perceive tennis shoes, watches, and personal electronics in generally similar ways. But these circumstances are quite rare. In almost every other case, exporting alone dramatically limits and reduces the ability of a company to grow its business worldwide.

The idea that the global marketplace is the sole domain of large multinationals must change. Way too many smaller companies are missing the opportunities afforded by global manifest destiny and relying only on exporting as *the* way to create a global presence. Some businesses are not interested in moving beyond exporting because they feel too comfortable. This is a dangerous position to take because the global economy—with its accelerating pace of change and ever-newer information technology—brings competition from unexpected places. Thus, smaller businesses are not always safe and stable within their supposed domestic niches.

On the surface at least, all the ingredients for small and midsize companies successfully going global are there. But it's not that easy: There are real challenges, and it takes real discipline. Many smaller companies are not necessarily interested in introducing that much discipline into their organizations and their decision making. And when a company makes a mistake in going global, the results can be expensive, in both financial outlays and failed opportunity costs.

GLOBAL MANIFEST DESTINY AND AMERICANIZATION

At this moment, an important point must be made. With all due respect to the strength of the United States as the leading player on the world's economic stage today, globalization is not simply the Americanization of the world's population. Globalization is much deeper and more profound than the influence of solely one nation or culture. Just as the Europeans, Chinese, Africans, Romans, Greeks, Egyptians, and Phoenicians before them, the Americans of today are merely the most visible, yet unknowing, flag bearer of globalization. The Europeans and Romans, for example, probably dominated more of the world and were the unaware carriers of the flag in their day. Certainly, these cultures influenced the course of events for a much longer period of time than the United States has.

In fact, the best place to view the integration of the world's people today is not in North America, Western Europe, Japan, or other industrialized nations, but in what is commonly referred to as the emerging markets of the world. The magnitude and ferocity of economic integration in places such as Almaty, Mumbai and Timbuktu is striking to even the most seasoned observer of globalization. In these and countless other places like them, billions of people are becoming economically integrated with their global counterparts for the very first time in an increasingly rapid fashion.

THE TREMENDOUS OPPORTUNITIES IN EMERGING MARKETS

Our first book, entitled *Growing Your Business in Emerging Markets: Promise and Perils* (Quorum Publishing, 2000), details both the inherent risks and tremendous opportunities in doing business in emerging markets. It is not our intention to rewrite that book here; nevertheless, it is critical to recognize the importance of these opportunities. They provide another compelling reason why a company needs to achieve a global presence.

The spectacular economic growth in emerging markets is the beginning of the biggest consumer boom in history. More customers with more income than ever before will provide manufacturers and distributors with the greatest moneymaking opportunity in the Industrial Age. In short, the place to strike it rich is in the emerging markets of the world and the time is now.

In comparison to the industrialized nations, emerging markets over the past 20 years have been growing at an increasingly faster rate. Throughout the developing world, annual population growth, crude birth rates, and fertility rates are all dramatically higher than in developed countries. In Latin America and Africa, the fertility rates among women are nearly three times higher than in Western Europe and the United States. An average Latin woman will produce five children in her lifetime, while an average African woman will deliver nearly six. The expanding, large populations of emerging markets are being coupled with a dramatic rise in per-capita income in some markets as evidenced by rapid economic growth. For the year 2000, the gross domestic product (GDP) in most regions of emerging markets grew at a faster rate than that of Britain, Japan, or even the United States. Moreover, every Asian region within emerging markets exceeded the 2000 growth of Japan, the region's biggest economy. Japan's GDP rose by 1.4 percent for 2000, versus 5.9 percent for western Asia, 7.95 percent for eastern and southern Asia, and 7.7 percent for China.

According to the Organization for Economic Co-Operation and Development (OECD), the forecast for economic growth in the developing world is projected at 5 percent annually over the next ten years. If China, India, Pakistan, Brazil, and Indonesia grow by an average of 6 percent per year through the year 2010 (still well below their projections of 8 percent to 10 percent annual growth), approximately 900 million people will live in those countries, with an income equivalent to that of the average American household. This group would represent the combined populations of the United States, the European community, and Japan.

THE BUSINESS PHASES OF GLOBAL MANIFEST DESTINY

From a business perspective, global manifest destiny has traditionally revealed itself in one of two forms: first, as a period of rapid growth, high sales, and oftentimes, but not always, high profits. Additionally during this period, there is heightened competition for limited resources and arrogance on the part of customers, suppliers, governments, etc., and constructive partnerships among and between customers, suppliers, and governments are relatively low. Also, a specific infrastructure and unique behavioral mode of collective thinking and actions prevail. This is the accelerated reactivity phase of global manifest destiny.

Conversely, the contrasting second period of slower economic growth of global manifest destiny is characterized by comparatively lower sales and profits, reduced competition for limited resources, i.e., a talent pool of workers, much easier compliance on the part of customers, suppliers, and governments, with a bias for more constructive alliancing and partnerships. During this time, a very different, but equally specific, infrastructure dominates and a very different mode of behavior prevails. This is the *decelerated proactivity* phase of global manifest destiny.

The phase of *accelerated reactivity* is usually the time when companies most often build greater profits. The pace of business is usually faster and more subject to wild fluctuations in the marketplace than during the decelerated proactivity phase. The accelerated reactivity phase typically reveals higher growth rates in both sales and profits than does the decelerated proactivity phase.

As the vast majority of companies during the accelerated reactivity phase see their profits increase, often at astounding rates, a premium is placed on resources that become increasingly scarce. This scarcity and the resulting higher cost of resources place an increasingly heavier burden on the existing infrastructure to create more of what is needed to sustain the accelerated reactivity phase. During this time, few people seek to improve the infrastructure. The primary focus is on generating higher profits and not to proactively pay attention to what is most certain to follow: the eventual ramping down and conclusion of the accelerated reactivity phase. Individuals and organizations merely react to what is going on around them, comfortable with the current climate. The inevitable overstressing of the inadequate then-current infrastructure in the accelerated reactivity phase is typically the ultimate catalyst for the inevitable transition to the decelerated proactivity phase.

Once the high profits and relatively easy money begin to evaporate, priority is placed on fixing the infrastructure and trying to return to the accelerated reactivity phase. Enlightened organizations attempt to repair and minimize the shortcomings of the current system and proactively build new infrastructures during these times of economic deceleration. For these enlightened companies, the decelerated proactivity phase is the time to keep and build market share first. Once market share is secured, these firms then extend focus on profits.

Events in Southeast Asia in the late 1990s illustrate the phases of global manifest destiny. From the late 1980s onward, many East Asian "tiger" economies were viewed as can't-miss opportunities for foreign investors. International lenders bankrolled everything from empty highrises in Bangkok to South Korean companies' speculation in Brazilian bonds. Sakura Bank Limited and Bank of Tokyo-Mitsubishi led a long line of Japanese banks that more than doubled their lending to Thailand between 1993 and 1996. Germany's Deutsche Bank made risky temporary loans across Russia and the Commonwealth of Independent States (CIS) as well as Asia so it could be first in line for corporate bond deals. "All the banks would be standing in line—J.P. Morgan, Deutsche, CitiBank, Dresdner," said Klaus Friedrich, chief economist at Germany's Dresdner Bank. "We were all queuing up, trying to help those countries borrow money. We would all see each other in the same places. We all knew each other."

Beginning in early 1995, however, fast-track economies like those of Indonesia, South Korea, Thailand, and Malaysia, each characterized with loosely controlled banking systems and political corruption, began to experience a decrease in their amount of annual growth. The slowdown in the revenue stream made it increasingly difficult for the "tigers" to pay back the Japanese banks and other international investors who had financed their fantastic growth over the previous years.

Nevertheless, governments and business leaders in these countries, as well as the foreign lenders who were providing the much-needed capital, failed to recognize the natural shift that was occurring and continued to behave as if they were still at the beginning of the accelerated reactivity phase, rather than at the end of it.

The behavior of leaders in Thailand during the early 1990s typifies what happened in many other countries throughout

Southeast Asia. The nation launched its own satellites, constructed taller skyscrapers, built automobile plants faster than highways were laid, and expanded its telecommunications network at a record pace.

By the time first-time visitors arrived at their hotel from the Bangkok airport, they all were asking the same question, "Where did all of the money come from?" Most of the megaprojects were financed with so much overseas money that during the boom times, the political and economic shortcomings within the system could be covered up. As the returns on these foreign investments shrank, however, cracks started to appear in the local economies.

The needed discipline on the part of the country's political and financial leaders was nowhere to be found. Politicians kept on promoting the promise of Thailand and constantly sought to lure foreign firms to set up shop there, regardless of the real needs of the marketplace. In one six-month period during 1995, three new tractor factories and four new automobile plants broke ground. Nobody stopped to ask if a demand existed to sustain these new facilities. Instead, the focus was on the development and the development alone. Thailand's financial sector continued to lend money, assuming real estate values would only appreciate. Words such as *depreciation* and *negative equity* were alien concepts to a generation of Thai bankers accustomed to annual growth rates of 8 percent to 10 percent.

As the cracks became more visible in 1996 and early 1997, rumors about a correction to the Thai economy started to spread as international investors began to call for the Thai economy to increase its productivity, lower wages, and deal with the banking sector.

When faced with these demands from their financial benefactors, Thai leaders proved impotent in addressing the concerns. On July 2, 1997, the Thai government, under tremendous pressure from international lenders, stopped using public funds to peg the baht to the U.S. dollar. Currency speculators and investors immediately pulled their money out of Thailand and the other countries of the region.

Two months later, Thailand became the first Asian country to appeal to the International Monetary Fund (IMF) for short-term loans to maintain its economy. In Japan, political leaders remained unable to agree on how to revive the beleaguered banking system. While on Wall Street, fears of an Asian recession forced the Dow Jones Industrial Average to fall more than 557 points on October 27, 1997.

Soon, other nations, such as South Korea, Indonesia, the Philippines, and Malaysia, found themselves in the same dire situation as Thailand. The failing economies created political and social unrest—particularly in Indonesia. Lenders and investors who were slow to pull out their money were harder hit, as the situation seemed to be spinning out of control.

In mid-1998, international investors began to realize that this Asian flu might spread to other emerging markets. In Russia, President Boris Yeltsin turned to the IMF for help. The fund loaned out billions of dollars, but it did little to help the sagging ruble. Brazil's economy imploded as the real was floated, falling more than 30 percent in value within a week. By the end of the year, the world became aware of the possibility of a massive economic downturn fueled by increasingly accelerated fear.

The culmination of these events was the inevitable movement into today's decelerated proactivity phase. Nevertheless, opportunities still exist. These opportunities, however, are new and different from the ones that existed in the preceding accelerated reactivity phase. As previously discussed, market share expansion is a key component of the decelerated proactivity phase. With proper strategies, enlightened companies can increase their international presence and build the necessary infrastructure for the next inescapable round of accelerated reactivity. Muthiah Alagappa, a Malaysian scholar at the East-West Center in Honolulu, best describes the current situation when he says, "This

[Asian situation] is a crisis, but also a tremendous opportunity for Western companies. The situation strengthens the position of Western companies in Asia." Jeffrey Garten, dean of the Yale School of Management, adds, "Most of these countries are going to pass through a deep and dark tunnel. But on the other end there is going to be a significantly different world, and it will be one in which Western firms have achieved much deeper penetration." Such an example distinguishes the transition between phases of global manifest destiny.

Moving back and forth between the phases of decelerated proactivity and accelerated reactivity is often not a clean, uniform and painless transformation. Some industries will change phases faster or slower than others will. Certain countries will rise or fall before their neighbors do. And a few companies will often be able to adjust to the natural changes of global manifest destiny much smoother than their competitors do.

Those companies that adapt their cultures to better leverage the advantages afforded them in each of the inevitable phases and transitions of global manifest destiny will undoubtedly be the leaders in their respective universes. Those business leaders, organizations, and financial investors who will succeed in the new millennium are those who seize the initiatives that each phase of global manifest destiny offers.

The following chapters will provide a road map that is designed to help business leaders understand their key business functions in better fulfilling their company's global destiny.

We will explore global culture, global marketing, global account management, global customer service, global e-business, global procurement, global operations, and global finance. We will examine many of the characteristics of these critical business processes and provide a blueprint of how a business leader can develop a global-based strategy for each of these areas.

The illustrations in this book come from a wide range of companies and industries. Many are experiences of larger companies. While this book is written primarily for smaller and mid-size firms, we feel that much can be learned—both what to do and what not to do—from large multinationals.

We sincerely hope that the following chapters will provide you with the real-world, hard-hitting insight necessary to take full advantage of the world that global manifest destiny has created. To start with, we'll begin by looking at what global culture is and how a company can develop a strategy to integrate itself within an ever-expanding global marketplace.

CHAPTER 2

GLOBAL CULTURE

I n our many years of working with companies that are attempting to move beyond merely exporting, we have witnessed far
too many organizations that try to force-feed a global culture
to their domestic organizations. They often do this by creating an
international sales department, or by expanding their export office, or by requiring certain staff members to take Spanish language courses. None of this seems to work. It comes up short in
the face of both the demands and opportunities afforded by
global manifest destiny.

These activities most often further an inability to leverage
ideas developed in one country to other countries worldwide.
Innovations developed in one country stay locked in the country
of origin. Moreover, these efforts often create an us-versus-them
cultural and operational divide within an organization. By its
very nature, such an approach usually results in the development of the "international branch" versus the domestic or "main
business" of a company.

WHAT IS GLOBAL CULTURE?

A *global corporate culture* is a system of shared goals, values, and behaviors. A global culture is often characterized by the following:

- Indifference to nationality, race, color, creed

- Respect for cultural differences

- Shared core values

- A behavioral as well as a common lingua franca

A global culture is an assimilation of the best characteristics of a wide variety of individuals from diverse backgrounds who feel they are actively encouraged to contribute to the greater goals of the company. It is an integration of these people, ideas, and innovations into the entire corporate culture.

Global culture is much more than a global mind-set. A global mind-set is primarily an appreciation of other cultures. Global culture involves using a global mind-set to develop a global strategic vision.

To create a global culture requires leadership that intuitively and viscerally embraces venturing into the global unknown and, moreover, possesses the strength and skills to take a company into the new global economy.

As researcher and author Robert Rosen discusses the development of "global literacies" in his book of the same name, he aptly defines *global* as "being world-class at home and abroad." Rosen goes on to define *literacies* as "new competencies for the new era." In his book, Rosen further articulates four components crucial to global leadership: being good global economists; thinking with an international mind-set; acting with fresh, global-centric behaviors; and mobilizing a world-class team.[1]

We agree with Rosen that an entirely new mind-set must be developed by leaders of hopeful global companies—a mind-set of global knowledge accumulation; a mind-set of personnel and personal internalization.[2] We call this the development of global-centric company culture.

DEVELOPING A GLOBAL CULTURE

Culture is a dynamic process for solving human problems as well as organizational problems. It is dynamic because it changes as circumstances change, and it has evolved in a way that is logical to the people inside that culture to help them solve their everyday problems.

Management books and articles are overwhelmingly developed and preached by business experts and gurus largely from the Anglo-Saxon world, and, unsurprisingly, their theories are filled with the cultural assumptions of that part of the world. As a result, many of their supposedly universal solutions are irrelevant to a large part of the globe.

Many of the world's organizations still run on a model of human relationships that is more akin to the traditional family than the functionally organized, formal, vision-led type of organization prevalent in the United States and Northern and Western Europe.

Yet outside of these places, business culture is often the opposite. Relationships are protected, even at the cost of bending or breaking rules. Authority is exercised directly, and the decision of the boss is seen as perfectly legitimate. Managers in these cultures (Latin, Asian, Arab, and African) ask: "What does the person who designed this system know about my business?" If they decide someone should be the new director, then the decision is theirs to make.

When people reach a certain level of awareness about the nature of cultural differences, they can begin to appreciate the benefits of another culture's point of view. Once different points of view are respected and considered equal, new ways of working together can develop. So long as individuals accept only the validity of their own view of the world, international business becomes a battle to get the Mexicans to follow the systems or to explain again to the Chinese that you are working to a deadline.

With respect for each other's logic, we start to look for ways to reconcile our different views of the world into an entirely new way of working that builds on the best features of each culture. Reconciliation is not compromise—it is creating a rich new synthesis that is more valuable than either of the preceding approaches. It is not a pale average.

Culture—that amalgam of tradition, relationships, and values—shapes business practices and processes in widely varying ways. Cultural differences often make it hard to obtain consensus and collaboration. The issue is a complex problem with no uniform solution. The gap between culture, business, and the required knowledge to effectively execute business processes can be tremendous. Closing this gap requires an understanding of one's own culture as well as the culture of others.

Real global leaders must deeply understand and appreciate cultural diversity, i.e., diversity of leadership style, industry style, individual behaviors and values, race, religion, and sex, to lead the development of globally minded cultures within their organizations. They need to know both the economic and legal differences between markets, as well as the social and motivational differences that are essential elements of conducting business around the world.

Leaders become more global in their thinking by formulating a clear and cogent global vision that they can communicate to a wide range of audiences around the world and that can inspire and motivate employees and investors around the word. This global vision also serves as the basis for building an internationally competitive top team composed of people who not only possess the direct experience and cross-border and cross-cultural competencies to do business in all markets of the world, but who can facilitate the transfer of ideas everywhere in the world.

Three ways companies can construct an effective and transparent global-centric culture include: (1) understanding the critical role of leadership; (2) integrating different ideas, concepts, and processes; and (3) recognizing the relationship between global culture and global behavior.

Understanding the Critical Role of Leadership

Corporate leaders must communicate that they are open to people in every country; that they can successfully engage in multilateral alliances to commit their firms to long-term interdependent relations, and that in the process they can find shared values with all the stakeholders.

Many leaders in the 21st century globally envision finding a leadership position in all the main geographical areas of the Americas, Europe, Middle East, Africa, and Australasia, and optimizing what can be learned in each area for customers everywhere.

To pursue their global vision, they need to understand in real time the political, economic, sociocultural, technological, and ecological forces in all these areas. Then, from studying the changing needs of customers and from the strategies of competitors everywhere in the world, they can begin to comprehend some aspects of the emerging global civilization. Their customers are people around the world who demonstrate through their preferences how they want to live. That there is a proliferation of Avon ladies in Brazil's Amazon and in China, where they number more than 600,000; that the travel industry is the world's largest; or that a Sambhuru warrior in northern Kenya can own a cellular telephone are but a few examples of this phenomenon. The growth of telecommunications and computer technologies not only connects the world more closely, it also creates a witness to global cultural shifts.

This transformation becomes evident in the premises that underlay the changes in the infrastructure of companies. This is currently described as a paradigm shift, with implications for changing visions, missions, systems of governance, strategy, organizational culture, and design. One specific change is that companies and their leaders must operate globally as well as aspire for insider status in an extraordinarily wide variety of cultural and national settings.

The following illustrations show how determined leadership can dramatically impact the development of a company's global culture.

Ranbaxy Pharmaceuticals. For almost 18 years after it began exporting, the Indian pharmaceutical company Ranbaxy remained trapped at the bottom of its industry. Even though the company had developed an advanced product and possessed the capabilities to sell in its domestic market, it had decided to expand globally by selling bulk substances to relatively unsophisticated markets. Because gross margins were between 5 percent and 10 percent, the additional revenue from the nondomestic business did not even offset the cost of the international sales and distribution. Like the management of so many companies all over the world, Ranbaxy's leaders justified the negative returns by celebrating the status and prestige associated with being a multinational and making vague promises about using overseas contacts and experience to upgrade their business.

This all changed in 1993, when the new chief executive officer, Parvinder Singh, challenged the top management with his dream of turning Ranbaxy into a truly global company. When posed with the question of how a small India company could compete with the rich giants from the United States and Europe, Singh responded by saying the company needed to develop a global culture that transcended India. "Ranbaxy cannot change

India. What it can do is to create a pocket of excellence. Ranbaxy must be an island within India."[3]

Once there was a shift in mind-set, led from the top, the next steps were straightforward. The company moved into higher-margin businesses like selling generics in large markets such as China and Russia. It then entered the United States and Western Europe. Each of these steps required new customer relationships, a strong brand image, and unique distribution channels. By using its increasing global knowledge and experience, the company was able to expand its capabilities and develop new resources. By 1996, more than half of the company's $250 million revenue came from outside of India.[4]

For companies anywhere, whether in the interior of India or on the East Coast of the United States, the lesson from Ranbaxy and others is clear: Getting out of the mind-set that a company cannot be a global player is one of the most important steps any firm can take to growing its business worldwide.

Ritz-Carlton. The approach taken by Ritz-Carlton at its new hotel in Shanghai illustrates how a company can successfully integrate its global culture.

Ritz-Carlton acquired rights to manage the property, with a staff of about 1,000 people, under its own name on January 1, 1998. The company's leadership believed that, consistent with its global culture, the operation would require significant upgrading. As expected, the company brought in a sizable contingent of about 40 expatriates from other Ritz-Carlton units around the world to transform and manage the new property.

Among its initial actions in the first week of operations under its own control, the company decided to start renovating from the employees' entrance rather than from other locations, like the main lobby. The logic of using this approach was that every employee would see two radical changes in the first week: One, that the new standards of quality and service would be dramatically higher; and two, that they, the employees, were among the most valued stakeholders in the company. This approach—not expensive, but incredibly effective—did more than anything else to communicate the company's culture to their employees: "We are ladies and gentlemen serving ladies and gentlemen."[5]

ResMed. ResMed is an Australia-based medical equipment company that specializes in treating a breathing disorder known as obstructive sleep apnea (OSA). Spun off in 1989 by U.S. giant Baxter, ResMed was a struggling start-up with revenues of just $1 million. By 1999, it was the world's number two competitor in the fast-growing market for OSA treatment devices, and its products were generating sales of $90 million a year.

The leadership of Dr. Peter Farrell, CEO of ResMed, was fundamental to the tremendous growth of the company. On becoming CEO, Dr. Farrell encouraged ResMed's research to build networks with other leaders in the international community. He led a team on a worldwide fact-finding tour of leading researchers and physicians and put together a medical advisory board to help ResMed develop its products to the industry standard.

More recently, Farrell launched a global campaign to encourage the medical profession to recognize the strong links between sleep-disordered breathing and the incidence of strokes and congestive failure. Farrell also moved the company's center of operations closer to the firm's largest and most sophisticated markets. In these and other ways, Farrell's leadership pushed the company to act like a leading global player long before that was an operating reality.[6]

Integrating Different Ideas, Concepts, and Processes

Many firms begin integrating different ideas, concepts, and processes from within. Following are illustrations of companies that applied these methods in constructing their companies' global cultures.

Clyde Bowers PLC. Clyde Bowers, a Scottish firm, had annual sales in 1999 of approximately $225 million. With 875 employees and operations in more than a dozen countries, the company works predominantly in the power sector, manufacturing boiler-cleaning equipment for power stations and materials-handling equipment. Its global activities range from marketing offices in seven countries to materials-handling joint ventures in India and China to soot-blower manufacturing in various countries, including Estonia.

Like its marketing, the firm's research and development is decentralized as well. Foreign nationals play a fundamental role in the company. Under 10 percent of employee turnover occurs in Scotland, although more than 12 percent of its employees are based there. This is the result of the company's recent history of growth through global acquisitions. Clyde Bowers now has moved from supplying 3 percent of the world boiler-cleaning market to 55 percent.

Activities are driven by the company's philosophy of being a global company with a dynamic global culture, operating in the places where it is cost-effective to do so and where it can be close to its competitors. Substantial links between the company and its host markets have been formed and all are integrated into corporate activity, particularly through the activities of their recently appointed Chief Knowledge Officer (CKO).[7]

Desc, S.A. A global vision on the part of a company's leaders has helped many a seemingly domestic or regionally focused firm become a global contender. Fernando Senderos Mestre took over running his father's company, Desc, S.A., in 1988, just as Mexico's economy was beginning to open up to foreign competition. Seeing that the world's auto-parts business was still too concentrated in industrialized markets, Mestre sought to leverage his company's competitive advantages—low labor cost and geographic proximity to the world's largest automobile market, the United States—over his global competitors.

In fostering a global culture, Mestre changed the traditional ways most Mexican firms had been operated, and went outside of Mexico for new staff and new ideas. He brought in engineers from Brazil, designers from Spain, and technical-support specialists from Japan. By 1999, Mestre had grown the company's annual sales to $2 billion—with more than half taking place outside of Mexico.

Quadstone. Quadstone is a company that spun out of Edinburgh University in 1995. It operates in the emerging global niche of data mining, a sophisticated computer technique used in targeted marketing. The Gartner Group, one of the premier market analysts in the information technology (IT) sector, placed Quadstone as number five in the world behind number one IBM. In the United Kingdom, Quadstone's clients include Barclays Bank, Sainsbury's, and Liverpool Victoria Group. Global business for Quadstone is the cornerstone, with the United States being their largest possible market.

Quadstone's global culture is unique because it retains its links to Scottish academia by sponsoring Ph.D. students within the company. Each intern is required to spend time in the each of the firm's main offices in Singapore, Frankfurt, and Boston. This exposure for its new employees makes it much easier for those same employees to partner with the company's global clientele and learn its customers' business.[8]

Televisa. Spanish-speaking soap operas are some of the most watched and most followed programs in the world. Their audiences are as loyal as any on the planet. Interestingly, however, almost two-thirds of all television programming—including most soap operas—in the Spanish-speaking world traditionally originate in the United States. It would seemingly be quite difficult for a Mexican company to stake its claim in this hypercompetitive market. Nonetheless, that is what Televisa has accomplished.

Unlike most U.S. programming that is homogenized for large populations and assumes that all Spanish speakers are culturally the same, Televisa sought to provide specific content for each particular cultural segment. The firm recognized that although an Argentine and a Panamanian may each speak Spanish, their cultural and linguistic differences are great. By hiring managers and writers from different countries and integrating them into a new culture, the Mexican firm was able to tailor programming for each Spanish-speaking country and therefore enhance its value position. As a result, the firm is now the largest producer of Spanish-speaking soap operas, or *novelas*, in the world.

Sometimes the best integration takes place when systems, ideas, and processes are brought in from the outside—even from competitors.

Jollibee's. Leaders of smaller companies with limited global experience obviously will be overwhelmed when facing the large multinationals in an unfamiliar setting. Yet, as already discussed, the economic integration of humankind is inevitable and unstoppable. The sooner a company realizes it, the better off it will be.

Jollibee's, a fast-food chain based in the Philippines, was written off by many when the giant McDonald's entered that country in 1981. Hardly anybody believed the 11-store chain would survive. Instead, Jollibee's has flourished, and grown its business worldwide. Like so many examples of smaller companies surviving and thriving in the face of seemingly impossible circumstances, Jollibee's owes much of its success to cultural integration. Unlike other leaders who might have turned tail and run, CEO Tony Tan Caktiong saw McDonald's entry into his market as an opportunity to train his people on how to be a world-class organization.

Going up against a formidable global company gave everyone at Jollibee's a firsthand perspective of the fantastic operating systems that McDonald's uses to control quality, costs, and service. So, in many ways, Jollibee's was able to integrate the culture of McDonald's into its own business. Moreover, Jollibee's developed menus to rival McDonald's that were customized to local tastes. Along with noodle and rice meals made with fish, Jollibee's created a seasoned burger with garlic and soy sauce, which helped the company capture nearly 75 percent of the burger market and more than two-thirds of the fast-food business in the Philippines. Having learned what it takes to compete with a global company, Jollibee's gained the confidence to go global. Using its recipes and systems that were integrated from McDonald's, the company has established dozens of restaurants in Hong Kong, the Middle East, and California.[9]

Indah Kiat Pulp & Paper (IKPP). From Indonesia, Indah Kiat Pulp & Paper (IKPP) has aggressively moved into global markets by drawing on a ready supply of logs—the product of favorable growing conditions and low harvesting costs. IKPP's cost advantage, however, is not entirely due to geography. The company has also invested heavily in advanced machinery to make its production more efficient. Rather than being content to let resources provide the sole advantage, companies like IKPP have measured themselves against the practices of leading global companies in their industry. By moving toward the productivity, quality, and service levels of global competitors and integrating this mind-set in the culture, even small companies in commodity industries like IKPP are able to build a sustainable basis for long-term global success.[10]

Recognizing the Relationship between Global Culture and Global Behavior

Companies that are concerned with their reputations—and that's nearly all companies—recognize that they have to focus on their global principles.

Ignoring global ethical issues can even cost a firm customers at home. There is evidence that if consumers know that a company is unethical anywhere in the world, they will exercise their disapproval at the cash register.

The belief that moral values such as openness and trust are such integral parts of successful capitalism was even held by capitalism's "founder," Adam Smith. Before writing his *Wealth of Nations*, Smith penned a treatise arguing that for capitalism to work it must be based on shared rules and common values.

Most international business practitioners would probably admit that the issue of bribes has arisen at some point in their career. Whether by a local customs official or an employee of a distributor, bribes seemingly play a large role in the conduct of global business.

In addition to the issue of bribes and tax-free markets, two other areas are increasingly coming under the hot glare of ethics watchers: human rights and the environment. American consumers may not get too worked up over gifts to foreign partners or government officials, but they will quickly show their displeasure at the thought of mistreated—especially underage—workers and toxic waste polluting pristine waters and wildernesses around the world.

Levi Strauss. Even an ethically sensitive company such as Levi Strauss can find rough sailing when navigating international human rights. The company won great praise for its handling of a child-labor charge at its Bangladesh plants in 1992. The company discovered soon after it had stepped up its campaign to monitor foreign plants that two sewing subcontractors employed young children—a norm in a country where kids without jobs frequently beg or prostitute themselves for money. The firm cleverly solved the problem by having the contractors remove the children from the factory but continue to pay their wages on condition that they attend school full-time. When they reached the local maturity age of 14, they were guaranteed getting their jobs back.

How does a company doing business internationally navigate these ethical storm waters? It does so, according to the experts, by implementing a true ethics program with teeth, not by merely trotting out a piece of paper, and by recognizing that despite cultural differences, certain core ethical values are held by all people around the globe.

Honeywell. At Minneapolis-based Honeywell Inc., with nearly half its employees located outside the United States, senior management regularly emphasizes ethics in its regional newsletters. One such publication for the Asia-Pacific, for example, carried a message from the president that the company would prefer to lose business rather than succumb to paying a bribe. An ethics advice line encourages employees to discuss ethical decisions they are unclear about. The company, which recently rewrote its code to be less focused on the United States and more applicable globally, also conducts training around the world. The code's various aspects, from child-labor issues to gifts and gratuities, are enumerated specifically in its code of ethics handbook.

Honeywell has put teeth into its ethical principles by making adherence to the company's code a condition of employment, thus alerting employees that top management takes this topic seriously. Other companies take the opposite approach, basing employee compensation in part on adherence to ethical codes.

A WORD ABOUT ETHICS

The realities of global business compel business leaders to examine the ethical issues facing their companies in a variety of situations.

Throughout the developing world, many high-end goods are readily available through thriving contraband markets. Ask any world traveler which city is the largest center for commercial goods, and you'll get several educated guesses: Hong Kong, Miami, Dubai. Each is a good try but not even close; it is Ciudad del Este in eastern Paraguay. More than $20 billion a year in consumer goods move in and out of this city of 45,000 people.

The reason is simple: pragmatism. Every morning, the two bridges that connect Ciudad del Este with Iguaçu, Brazil, are filled with buses of Brazilians coming to shop and avoid the ridiculously high 80 percent import duties charged on all imported goods into Brazil. On arrival into Ciudad del Este, each bus is met not by Paraguayan immigration or customs official but by eight-year-old children selling duffel bags. The Brazilian shoppers dismount the buses, buy the duffel bags, and spend the next six hours filling them with every possible item they can buy—Chinese radios, Japanese VCRs, American handguns, Korean televisions, French champagne, and Italian suits. After the shopping spree is over, the buses reload and are visited by Paraguayan officials who wish the departing Brazilians well and extract their daily salary through the collection of "export duties." Once back home on the other side of the bridge, Brazilian customs officials replicate the work of their Paraguayan counterparts by demanding "import duties." Of course, each shopper's tax bills are only a fraction of what the official taxes would be in Paraguay and Brazil.

Tax-free markets like Ciudad del Este have been used extensively by companies to build product and brand awareness. One of the largest automobile manufacturers in the world reports 20 percent of its total earnings in Latin America comes from its spare-parts center in Ciudad del Este. Remembering that the fundamental goal is to get the product to market, a great majority of firms have viewed the underground economy as a necessity, without regard for the perceived moral or ethical elements of this activity.

Not too long ago, the global market leader in a particular industry, a U.S.-based Fortune 500 company; the number-two player worldwide, a UK-based firm; and the fourth-largest competitor, another U.S.-based Fortune 500 company, were each deciding how to best sell their products in the Chinese market.

After each company engaged in the necessary steps to evaluate the realities of the marketplace, two distinct strategies emerged. First, the number-one and number-two market leaders decided to establish a token presence with a series of small offices throughout China to provide the necessary "cover" for their marketing and merchandising activities. These local offices were never intended to serve any real purpose, except to assure local authorities that they were conducting normal and customary business.

Unbeknownst to local Chinese authorities, however, the vast majority of real business for both of these companies was being done *vis à vis* tax-free markets. Instead of importing the goods through a joint-venture partner, most of the commercial activity for these two firms took place through the porous border with Russia. Goods crossed with little or no interference, and, therefore, much less customs duties.

Second, the number-four market leader decided to take the more traditional approach by working directly with the Chinese government and entering into a joint venture purchase of an existing factory.

The differences in revenues were truly unbelievable. The market leader earned about U.S.$500 million in annual revenues from its back-door operation in China. The second-leading firm using the same approach earned about U.S.$425 million each year. The more traditional competitor never made more than U.S.$5 million in any of the four years it was in China. Who's right, who's wrong? You make the call.

More often than not, governments play a major role in sales and distribution within emerging markets. Protectionist import duties, state control of public distribution systems, and state-run companies are all used by national governments to control product development within its borders.

Although free trade and antiprotectionism are the stated policies of most governments in the world, high import taxes are still placed selectively on products to protect local industries. Antidumping laws in the United States—the world's most vocal supporter of free trade—still place a 45 percent tax on certain goods like ball bearings and textiles to protect American jobs. Brazil, in order to protect its local automobile manufacturers, levies a 125 percent import tax on all non-Brazilian models. As a result, less than 1 percent of Brazil's 250,000 annual automotive sales are from imported units.

The control of the Indian government over the distribution of alcoholic beverages is a classic case of state authority. In a country of nearly one billion people, it's remarkable that only 22,500 licensed shops and 10,000 other outlets are permitted to sell liquor. All points of sale must be licensed, including wholesalers, retailers, bars, restaurants, and bonded warehouses. Further, licenses from both the central government and an individual state are required. To complicate the process, controls on distribution vary from state to state and enforcement rights are held by either the government or auctioned to private companies. A simple change in the product, such as the alteration of the size of the bottle, can result in never-ending bureaucratic hassles.

Given the different laws and taxes applied by the various entities, marketers spend much of their time trying to figure out the rules. Import duties, export taxes, excise charges, and vendor fees are applied in various ways at any given moment. On top of the official regulations for alcohol distribution, a Mafia syndicate in Russia with strong political connections has emerged to shake down alcohol marketers and a take a piece of the action. The combination of these factors discourages innovation and reinforces the status quo.

To do any business in Russia, a company needs to have a roof, or *kriesha*, which provides cover from the harsh elements of the new, free-market system there. There are essentially two kinds of *kriesha*: government sponsored or criminal sponsored. Each of these provides shelter against the other, which is constantly trying to muscle its way into a given enterprise. For a percentage of the profits, a *kriesha* will use its influence to protect the company from either the local political authorities or Mafia syndicate.

In China, foreign companies are forced to use the state network and find their marketing approaches severely restricted. Within the major cities, Chinese state systems, not independents, distribute Coca-Cola and Procter & Gamble products. Control over distribution, therefore, tends to remain in the hands of communist bureaucrats.

As we all learned in elementary school, it is better to work together than against one another. Creating partnerships with the government can be a preferred way in which to overcome the obstacles to conducting business in emerging markets. A leading soft-drink maker partnered with the Moscow Metropolitan System by providing mobile carts and kiosks to offer soft drinks and snacks. The Moscow Metro—the largest underground transportation system in the world—viewed the protocol with the Western firm as a way to expand customer service. The end result was a joint venture between the two and the establishment of the Metro Express.

It goes without saying that the bribing of local officials is another way in which to influence the distribution process. A recent World Bank survey of 3,600 firms in 69 countries showed 40 percent of businesses pay bribes. In industrial countries, it was 15 percent and in the former Soviet Union, it had climbed to more than 60 percent.

In Russia, like most of the former Soviet Union, the last two weeks of each month see a dramatic rise in the number of "gifts" made to local police officials. Caslione is no longer surprised when he sees the driver enter his car with a stack of *ruble* notes in anticipation of the gifts we will pay out at every intersection on the way from the hotel to the distributor's office.

The lobby of the Sheraton in Caracas is one of the world's great meeting centers for foreign businesspeople interested in providing gifts to the right person. Venezuelan officials, seemingly unconcerned about the public atmosphere of the hotel, collect plain brown envelopes from foreigners in between shots of whiskey and bottles of Polar beer. On more than one occasion, so many "meetings" have been arranged at the same time, it has been necessary for the foreign businessperson to pay a little extra something to the hotel staff in order to ensure a couple seats in the lobby.

The ultimate decision of how to conduct global business is up to each company and the people who lead it. To help set parameters, we included the following guidelines to help leaders better evaluate the impact of ethical decisions on their companies.

Guidelines for Making Global Business Ethics Decisions

If the answer to any of these questions is "yes," the behavior or activity should be reevaluated and reexamined by the key decision makers of the firm.

1. Would any of the company's key stakeholders (employees, shareholders, upper management, strategic suppliers, or customers) be embarrassed if he or she found out about this behavior?

2. Would any of the company's key stakeholders immediately disapprove of this behavior?

3. Would any of the company's key stakeholders feel that this behavior is unusual?

4. Would any of the company's key stakeholders be upset if this activity or behavior happened to them?

5. Are decision makers concerned about the possible consequences of this behavior? Is there active or ongoing discussion about the ramifications of the behavior?

6. Would strategically important customers be upset if this behavior or activity were publicized in a newspaper or Internet article?

7. Would this behavior spill over into other aspects of the business and negatively impact the corporate culture?

Again, these are only guidelines for ethical behavior. The final decisions will be made by your company.

SUMMARY

A global culture is an assimilation of the best characteristics of a wide variety of individuals from diverse backgrounds who feel they are actively encouraged to contribute to the greater goals of the company. It is an integration of these people, ideas, and innovations into the entire corporate culture.

CHAPTER 3

GLOBAL
MARKETING

In the past, most companies' desire to deliver customer value
(or at least perceived customer value) was driven largely by a
domestic model or approach, which relied primarily on a standardized product and service portfolio strategy to create their
international or export marketing approach. Multiple products
and services, multiple markets, multiple geographies, multiple
income streams—sometimes they're related, but often they're not.
Portfolios worked, and worked well, as long as markets were
geographies with rules, customs, and known competitors. But in
a global system, there are glaring problems with this model and
significant consequences for not getting it right.

Historically, global marketing organizations have grown
from a domestic base, which is natural. That is, they took the
same products or services they marketed domestically to other
countries. There, they usually attempted to replicate the domestic structure and the same company orientation. Thus, most global
sales and marketing organizations have evolved from their domestic models.

WHAT IS GLOBAL MARKETING?

For most companies, future success in marketing will come from a global marketing orientation, that is, recognizing that customers are customers no matter where they are. Core global marketing approaches suggest success will come from being the best in the world at what the company does, not just the best in the market, category, or geographic area. A global company operates with resolute constancy—at low relative cost—as if the entire world (or major regions of it) were a single entity.

This new emerging model of global marketing is called *global-local* or, for short, *glo-cal,* because its goal is to merge global strategy with deference for local needs. An example of a company recognizing the critical need to more closely tie marketing execution to the creation of global brand portfolios is Procter & Gamble. This U.S.-based, global, consumer products leader launched a new initiative called Organization 2005 to transform itself from a U.S. company doing business in 140 countries to a truly global company. Organization 2005 created a road map for P&G to transform itself from four geographically organized businesses into seven product category–based businesses. Baby-care merchandise is handled by a single business unit worldwide, while the other like-structured P&G divisions are each set up to handle the remaining product categories, i.e., beauty care, fabric and home care, feminine protection, food and beverages, and health care.[1]

The key for any company, of any size, seeking to become global is to be global and local at the same time. People don't think of themselves as global consumers, so companies can't think that way, either.

Global marketing focuses on global similarities rather than multidomestic differences. In short, global marketing is integrated. Integrated global marketing leads a company toward a new set of global capabilities—a new way of looking at the organization and what it does—not "better at what the organization does now" or not "improvements on current policies and systems and approaches."

To really achieve a global focus, an organization must become skilled at developing processes and systems that integrate the entire organization horizontally and around the world, not just better at enhancing traditional vertical skills and capabilities. Marketing in particular has to become more adept at resource allocation and measurement of returns. In short, marketers must become asset, customer, and resource managers, not just allocation and distribution managers.

Most of all, with a global organization, a different type of leader is needed to execute a global marketing strategy. This is the same kind of person described in the previous chapter. This person is equally at home in all national cultures. This person understands and manages the developing global culture, is adept at leading and learning quickly, and can teach effectively.

At one time marketers entering international or global positions were often viewed as moving sideways and then, a few months later, quietly shuffling out of the company. Not anymore. Today, businesses are looking at increasing globalization of everything from the manufacturer of their products to their purchasing of raw materials. And getting experience at an international marketing role is now seen as a precursor to a more senior management position within many companies. The world of marketing has changed and with it many of the skills demanded of marketers.

There is now a level of global marketer whose perspective extends to an entire world, not just to one or two whole continents. With the job comes genuine new responsibility. Unfortunately, not enough people are available to fill the roles required. There's rocketing demand for international competence but very little supply. The number of companies that need to build their brands in more than one country is snowballing across the United States.

In a study conducted by the Massachusetts Institute of Technology (MIT) in Cambridge, researchers found that 29 percent of the companies surveyed had "nowhere enough global leaders," and 56 percent stated that they had "fewer global leaders than needed."[2] Despite the many documented successes of U.S. companies in driving business in the global marketplace over the past 50 years, a quick tally of the numbers reveals that more than 80 percent of the companies surveyed stated that they were lacking the global leaders they believed they needed in their companies. If this isn't distressing enough, the study goes on to state, "Companies say that developing competent global leadership is the most important critical resource for achieving future global business success, [but] fully 85 percent of those firms lack global leaders today."[3]

Exacerbating the problem is a severe shortage of available business leaders in all functions of business, not just marketing, with meaningful and substantive international experience and skills in all cultures, although awareness of the need certainly is growing. While marketing is always in a state of transition, the rapidly changing and evolving new profiles of global marketing success in the new global economy are placing intense never-before-experienced pressures on global marketers.

Companies can move toward global marketing by comprehending the needs of local markets; blending collective needs into a global product and services portfolio; and making provisions for local market customs and consumer needs.

Global marketing is not conducting international business with the same concepts, approaches, products, and the like, adapted from or to local cultures and economies. These companies are organized along the national boundaries of the countries in which they have settled and operate, and they are focused on the cultures and issues of those locations. They produce products and services, then price, distribute, and promote them for that national market. These approaches have met with varying degrees of success along the way and sometimes even worked quite well for many organizations, particularly when these companies operated in markets with high barriers to competition or they realized major successes from their first-mover advantage. Regardless of their past successes, these companies are neither global thinkers nor global doers. They are still domestic in attitude and in action.

In recent years, this domestic approach has made it more difficult for these companies to cooperate with or join in the regional trading blocs that have emerged in the past decade, including the North American Free Trade Agreement (NAFTA), Mercosur, the European Union (EU), or the Commonwealth of Independent States (CIS), because of the differing goals, pricing structures, and cultures that exist within those regional economic trading blocs.

In addition, the rapid growth of the world economy has compelled companies to cross national and regional boundaries, cultures, economic systems, currencies, and so on—sometimes operating a bit out of control just to keep up.

DEVELOPING A GLOBAL MARKETING STRATEGY

The standardization versus adaptation debate has centered on the question of whether or not organizations should customize their domestic marketing strategies for global markets. Generally, standardization—using a common product, price, distribution, and promotion program on a global basis—is a more attractive strategy if markets or a company's product or service offerings are viewed as relatively homogeneous. With advances in technology, communication, and travel, which provide more global influences on consumers around the world, standardization of the basic marketing elements is fundamental to the introduction of products and services on a global scale. McDonald's and Coca-Cola use fairly similar marketing strategies, regardless of the country of operation.

Yet, this is much easier said than done, especially for smaller firms looking to create a global awareness of their products or services. Companies of all sizes must deal with multiple political, economic, legal, social, and cultural markets, as well as with various rates of change within each. In addition, the amount and quality of market research data—availability, depth, and reliability—varies a great deal among countries.

Following are some illustrations of companies who have either dealt with or failed to address these issues with regard to developing a global marketing strategy.

Merrill Lynch. After acquiring 2,000 employees from Yamachi Securities, Merrill Lynch & Company counted on an American-style investment advisor to build a high-trust image in the securities brokerage industry in Japan. Merrill Lynch missed the mark, however, because it failed to see to the cultural intricacies of the marketplace within the context of that particular market.

Historically in Japan, the securities industry has been tainted by unsavory practices. One well-known abuse is *churning,* in which salespeople persuade naive people to buy and sell a lot of securities so that salespeople can boost their commissions. Merrill Lynch promised that there would be no churning in its Japanese operation. Instead, its salespeople were to try to get an overall picture of the customers' finances, ascertain their needs, and then suggest investments. Something got lost in the translation, however. Japanese customers complained that Merrill Lynch salespeople were too nosy, asking questions instead of just telling them what stocks to buy. And, because of this, Merrill Lynch failed to overcome its domestic biases and look at the Japanese market from a non-American perspective.[4]

As this illustrates, obstacles to global cultural integration can come from a number of sources: local employees, local customers, local regulations, and so on. Given these obstacles, every company needs to clarify its core beliefs and practices. This clarity is essential for knowing where the company should stay committed and where it should be willing to adapt. Once this is established, the company needs to embed these beliefs and practices throughout its entire organization.

When attempting to establish a global marketing presence, a company must understand the uniqueness of the local market and decide which aspects of the firm's business model require little change, which require local adaptation, and which need to be reinvented. A company will face little need to adapt its strategy if it targets a customer segment in a foreign market similar to one in its domestic market. If the company wants to expand the customer base it serves in a new market, however, then adapting the business model to the unique demands of the local customers becomes mandatory.

Domino's Pizza. Domino's Pizza is a good example of a company that has benefited from more fully adapting its global marketing approach to local conditions when it entered India. Unlike Kentucky Fried Chicken, who entered India using its U.S. model and failed because of it, Domino's was successful because it tailored its marketing approach more to the Indian culture and lifestyle. Even though pepperoni pizza is one of the most popular items for Domino's in other markets, the company dropped it from the menu to show respect for the value Hindus place on the cow. Domino's also tailored other toppings, such as chicken, ginger, and lamb, to suit Indian taste buds.

The Peninsula Group. Hong Kong's luxury hotel chains—The Peninsula Group, The Regent, and Mandarin Oriental—are in the process of going global. Although the hotels have attained success in the rest of Asia rather quickly, winning over other markets like the United States has been harder. But at least one hotel has succeeded. In the short period of time since the start-up, the Peninsula in Beverly Hills has established itself as perhaps the premier hotel in all of the Los Angeles area. This success springs in great part from the Peninsula's ability to integrate the right critical capabilities, especially its immaculate service, while adding other local requirements, such as a stare-and-be-stared-at swimming pool complete with cabanas for Hollywood negotiations.[5]

THE CREATION OF GLOBAL BRANDS

Blending collective needs into a global product and services portfolio usually involves the creation of brands. Brands that capture both the hearts and minds of consumers are central to the concept of the global company.

Building a global brand requires more than just producing a great product or great service. To have impact internationally, companies must be in the market at the right times and at the right places with the right brands having global potential. In the Internet age, global brands are growing faster than ever. While it took Coca-Cola 100 years to get where it is now, McDonald's the best part of 50 years, and Nike 35 years, dot-coms seem to be able to establish a global brand in less than three. The Internet e-mail company, Hotmail, went from a good idea to 20 million clients and a $400 million sales price within 22 months.[6]

Consumer characteristics are becoming more widespread. One look at the globe will indicate that Beijing will soon be enormously similar consumer-wise to Boston, Berlin, Birmingham, and many other mainstream cultures. Less and less of this planet remains remote and untarnished by materialism. This very medium of communication—this book—will continue to shrink distances and mold people into larger and larger consumer units.

ACHIEVING WORLDWIDE ACCEPTANCE AND RECOGNITION

To achieve worldwide acceptance and recognition, manufacturers are constantly undertaking the following:

- Deciding which brands to make global

- Choosing a global brand name

- Repositioning their brands

- Creating global advertising campaigns

- Using point-of-sale (POS) or point-of-purchase (POP) advertising

- Crafting customer communications

- Building global brand alliances

- Translating foreign languages

Deciding Which Brands to Make Global

Even though most global brands are not absolutely identical from one country to another, companies whose brands tend be more global clearly reap some definite benefits. Yet, when a company decides to move from exporting to going global, it must decide whether it should globalize the entire portfolio simultaneously or only part of its product lines.

Marriott Hotels. Marriott, today the world's largest hotelier, was in the late 1980s essentially a domestic company. It had two principal lines of business: lodging and contract services. In addition to other activities, the lodging sector included four distinct product lines: full-service hotels and resorts (Marriott), midprice hotels (Courtyard), budget hotels (Fairfield Inn), and long-stay hotels (Residence Inn).

Contract services included the following three product lines: Marriott Management Services, Host/Travel Plazas, and Marriott Senior Living Services. As the company began its movement toward becoming a global contender, it had to decide which of its product lines should serve as the starting point for its global efforts. In other words, it had to decide where the "best bang for the buck" would come from.

Marriott successfully weighed this decision and focused its global marketing and branding efforts on its full-service lodging business. The company did so to serve globe-trotting corporate executives. In such a business, worldwide presence can create significant value by using a centralized reservation system, developing and diffusing globally consistent service concepts, and leveraging a well-known brand name that assures customers of high quality and service. In contrast, none of these factors is of high importance in the retirement community business, thus rendering this brand to its domestic-only status.

Choosing a Global Brand Name

Consumers and business customers in global marketing are humans and organizations with their own specific aspirations and culture. The way they perceive brands and marketing messages is vital to the success of the company marketing globally. A key factor for developing a successful global brand and establishing global brand equity is that the brand needs to be culture-proof. It needs to work across a wide range of languages, countries, and social situations.

Choosing a global brand name, however, brings its own problems. When spending on marketing communications and advertising, it is vitally important to make sure that the end result is well received by the people and organizations a company intends to make its customers.

The collective background, experience, and viewpoints of the nation's residents are unique to that particular place and moment in time. Like an individual, markets will each develop unique noticeable traits and behavior patterns that set them apart from all others. For example, a staunch Muslim nation such as Iran will certainly demonstrate a much different consumer personality than an ex-socialist country like a thriving Poland.

Functions of the nature of the collective background, experience, and viewpoints of a nation's residents are its attitudes and lifestyles. Global advertising campaigns are full of examples of noteworthy failures in the marketplace because of a failure to recognize specific aspects of a people's attitudes and lifestyles. The use of sexual images, sarcastic humor, and violence in advertising may play very well in one nation, while meeting stiff resistance in another. Throughout Africa and the Middle East, the depiction of women in advertising is more likely to be that of mother, friend, or care giver. In Latin America, on the other hand, women are portrayed in a sexual or flirtatious nature more often than not. This is true whether the advertisement is for a business product or service, or a consumer product or service.

People, their culture, their language, and their needs vary and must be taken into account carefully when developing a global marketing strategy. Otherwise, even creative and innovative, award-winning marketing in one market may quickly fail in another.

Repositioning Their Brands

Companies reposition their brands by seeking out ways of incorporating universal values in their marketing mix. The producer, whether it offers a physical product or a service, aims to connect consumer patterns from across the globe and refine these into an understandable image/reputation on a worldwide basis.

BRL Hardy. BRL Hardy is an Australian wine company that defied many of the well-entrenched traditions of international wine production and established a global brand.

In 1991, the company was exporting about $31 million of wine, much of it in bulk for private labels and the rest through myriad bottled products sold through distributors. Yet, by 1998, the company's nondomestic business accounted for $178 million—all sold as global brands.

Managing Director Steve Millar describes how the company started to make this happen: "We began to realize that for a lot of historical reasons, the wine business—unlike the soft-drinks or packaged-foods industries—had very few true multinational companies and therefore very few true global brands. There was a great opportunity, and we were as well placed as anyone to grab it."[7]

To create a global brand, the company hired staff and allocated resources to upgrade overseas sales offices. Moreover, instead of simply supporting sales and marketing activities of the overseas units, it took full control of sales, marketing, and distribution.

In addition, to fully leverage the marketing expertise of these overseas units, Hardy encouraged them to supplement their Australian product line by sourcing wine from around the world. Not only did this offset vintage uncertainties and currency risks of sourcing from a single country, it also gained clout in its relationships with retailers. By breaking the tradition of selling only its own wine, Hardy was able to build the scale necessary to create strong global brands.

The results have been outstanding. In Europe, for example, the volume of Hardy's brands has increased 12-fold, making it the number two brand in the huge UK market. In addition, Hardy's branded products from other countries have grown to represent about a quarter of its European volume.[8] Through the creation of global brands, Hardy has evolved from an Australian wine exporter to a truly global wine company.

Creating Global Advertising Campaigns

Global advertising campaigns are often centered on major events such as the Olympics or the World Cup Finals. Consumers from around the world are exposed as often as possible to the universal values possessed by the product or the service.

Federal Express. In applying its global marketing strategy to China, Federal Express had to choose whom to target: local Chinese companies or multinationals doing business in China. The company chose to target multinationals—a customer group that its global culture and business has been traditionally designed to serve. Given the choice, Federal Express was able to transfer the U.S. business model into China, including the use of its own aircraft, building a huge network of trucks and distribution centers, and adopting U.S.-style aggressive marketing and advertising.

Had FedEx selected local Chinese firms as its targeted customer segment, winning local customers would have required a significantly greater degree of local adaptation.

Using Point-of-Sale (POS) or Point-of-Purchase (POP) Advertising

Effective use of point-of-sale (POS) or point-of-purchase (POP) advertising extends the reach of global brand attributes and recognizes the local market's needs. It spreads both local customs/cultures and world values of the product, and establishes and reinforces the global brand.

Crafting Customer Communications

Using carefully crafted customer communications to present similar messages is a critical tool for all companies on a global scale. Big companies as well as their smaller counterparts now sponsor events that complement the message/image they want to portray. Firms of all sizes must recognize their social and ethical responsibilities and let their consumers know how they are meeting those responsibilities.

Global brands are brands whose positioning, advertising strategy, personality, look, and feel are, in most respects, the same from one country to another, especially within a rather homogeneous region. Global branding is the last step of the product identification stage in marketing management. Companies with an established brand in one country or region in the world can expand to a global basis. A company can use the same branding strategies it used to build awareness in any new market.

Building Global Brand Alliances

Global brand alliances can help tremendously to alleviate the financial investment necessary to enter a brand in any new market. This is especially true for smaller U.S.-based firms that have recently begun to explore the possibility of taking their domestic and exporting success to the next level. It may be even more daunting when taken to a multimarket and global level.

For example, a small U.S. manufacturer of medical equipment desiring to enter China had to make sizable investments to build brand awareness in that market. This same company has visions of expanding its brand presence to other markets in Asia-Pacific and Southeast Asia once the China business was firmly established.

In China alone, the company was faced with conducting an extensive communications campaign to build brand awareness and brand image, because of the sheer size of the market as well as China's fragmented infrastructure and the multiple language dialects in the different regions in China. In many cases, such a company might be dissuaded from introducing branded products in a targeted country market because of the commitment required to ensure success. If, however, a firm could identify methods of introducing brands that reduce the up-front costs of marketing and brand building, the probability of generating attractive returns might increase substantially. In this case, the U.S. company was able to successfully form a relationship with an alliance partner, a local Chinese company whose products complemented the U.S. company's product offerings and whose products' own brands were already well established. In this and other scenarios, developing strategic brand alliances in selected markets is a very viable alternative.

Clearly, cobranding is not a new idea in global marketing. Fuji-Xerox and the OneWorld Alliance between American Airlines/British Airways are examples of global firms jointly placing their brands in advertisements, promotion programs, and product/package labels to create entirely new and expanded value propositions for customers and consumers globally.

For smaller companies, brand allies may very well help to build consumer brand awareness and brand image for a fraction of the cost of building the global brand alone. Here's how:

- The ally's endorsement serves as a bond with the customer or consumer and aids in establishing credibility of the entering brand.

- The presence of an allied brand acts as an endorsement of the primary brand's quality.

- The initial investment requirements are much less.

Translating Foreign Languages

The literature is filled with examples of what can go wrong when U.S. businesses attempt to market their products abroad with less than an adequate grasp of the local language. When General Motors described its Body by Fisher in Flemish, it came out Corpse by Fisher, which did not increase sales. Pepsi-Cola's highly successful slogan "Come alive with Pepsi" almost appeared in the Chinese version of the *Reader's Digest* as "Pepsi brings your ancestors back from the grave." A U.S. airline operating out of Brazil tried to lure businesspeople by claiming it had plush "rendezvous lounges" in its first-class sections—without realizing that in Portuguese, the word *rendezvous* implies a room for making love.

Frank Perdue of Perdue Chicken fame decided to translate one of his successful advertising campaigns into Spanish with some unfortunate results. The slogan "It takes a tough man to make a tender chicken" was translated into Spanish as "It takes a virile man to make chicken affectionate."

As amusing as these may seem, such translation errors have cost U.S. companies millions of dollars, not to mention the damage to their credibility and reputations.

Young urban professionals in New York have more in common with their contemporaries in Singapore than with middle-class families on Long Island. The latter have more in common with people living in the affluent suburbs of Sydney.

The challenge for marketing professionals is to link their product to individual needs. Another is to create an idea for a single brand that transcends such differences by identifying it with an attitude or belief rather than a particular lifestyle that would be more market- and culture-specific.

Global brand equity is a result of successfully establishing global brand recognition, brand preference, and brand insistence. Global brand equity creates value for both the customer and the firm that is consistent and commonly recognized in markets throughout the world. These values are a result of firmly establishing global brand awareness and global brand association, and a perception of quality shared by customers in markets around the world.

A Caslione Client. While John Caslione was recently on-site with one of his multi-million-dollar clients headquartered in

Southern California, he couldn't help but admire the customer-service staff answering incoming calls. Directing this group was a customer-service manager who exemplified leadership for his global service team when he answered his first agent in English, the next in Spanish, followed by a quick conversation in French to another member of his team. All this from a customer-service manager who, as well as speaking four languages with consummate ease, also knew a lot about the technical aspects of the company's products. These same individual team members facilitate weekly team discussions to educate other team members about the specific customer needs and nuances for each of the markets that each individual team member represents.

This is an excellent illustration of a company that not only understands and values the cultures and languages of its target markets; it is also a company that actively and deeply involves all its people in further developing the core of the global corporate culture itself. Unlike many U.S. companies of its size that segment and separate the international business operations, this company integrates a multicultural and global approach into the organization from both a horizontal and a vertical perspective to execute on its global marketing strategy.

SUMMARY

A global marketing orientation is the recognition that customers are customers no matter where they are. Core global marketing approaches suggest success will come from being the best in the world at what the company does, not just the best in the market, category, or geographic area. A global company operates with resolute constancy—at low relative cost—as if the entire world (or major regions of it) were a single entity: It sells relatively the same core portfolio in the same way generally everywhere in the world.

This new emerging model of global marketing is called global-local or, sometimes for short, glo-cal, because its goal is to merge global marketing strategy with deference for local needs.

CHAPTER 4

GLOBAL ACCOUNT MANAGEMENT

These days, everyone wants to go global. At the same time, few really know the success formulas for global success. Success in domestic markets does not guarantee success in global markets. Success in global markets requires unique core business competencies that are not commonly required or developed in domestic markets.

When a domestic-based firm enters the global marketplace, it immediately meets two distinct groups of business challenges not faced at the domestic level.

RISKS GOING GLOBAL

The first group comprises the risks any business faces when entering global business:

- Financial risk, varying currency exchange, differential inflation, and divergent interest rates

- Political risk involving the potential for expropriation as well as other business harassment

- Regulatory risk arising from different legal systems, over-lapping jurisdictions, and dissimilar governmental policies

- Tax risk because of changes in fiscal policies affecting profitability

Dealing with this new set of risks requires a new learning curve that is not possible with domestic business models but instead must be acquired through actual global experience.

In addition to these inherent business risks shared by all global businesses, a second group of challenges is unique to global business development and sales. These challenges include:

- Setting up a global sales operation from scratch—a very time-consuming and even impossible exercise for some

- Duplicating many of the crucial factors in a company's domestic sales success that are difficult or almost impossible to do in global markets

- Establishing the important home-market advantages of a firm's dominant size, established market share, well-developed consumer recognition, plus all-important economics of scale for profitability that often are initially missing in new markets

- Overcoming these realities to build and maintain a global sales and service infrastructure

For all companies, regardless of their size or in what industries they work, to survive in the new global business arena they must often make the difficult and painful transition from a domestic company doing some international business to a primarily global company conducting true global business, including global account management. Moreover, most often an existing customer of a supplier who is either global, or seeking to become more global, becomes the catalyst or motivator for a company to seriously consider globalization.

Global account management, however, is not necessarily the same as global business development. Global business development relates to a company's ability to attract new business customers, of varying sizes and in a variety of industries, in foreign markets in which it is expanding, while global account management is the expansion of its business with current business customers as these customers expand their presence into new foreign markets.

Global account management generally mirrors a supplier company's existing national or key account management program that it has with its current domestic business customers, but now on a global scale. Pareto's Rule, commonly known as the 80/20 Rule, states that, with respect to sales volume, 80 percent of a business's sales is derived from a mere 20 percent of its customers—and these 20 percent are typically a supplier's largest domestic business customers. Extrapolating this same concept to a global level, more often a supplier's 80/20 customers are attempting to go global in their business and seek to have their existing supplier base support them in their global business development efforts. This support manifests itself in requests or demands that a continuing relationship is predicated on the supplier's ability to deliver products and services and support those products and services on a global basis to the now global customer. Failure to do so on the part of the supplier may, in fact, cause the supplier to not only lose the new global supply business opportunities, but also the current domestic supply business it has with its customer.

It is highly probable, then, that companies considering becoming global will do so in some way or in some shape, or as a result of business they are currently doing with one of their largest or most strategically important customers. Accordingly, it would be quite prudent that all companies begin to seriously consider their company's ability to understand and take on the challenges of true global account management. For most companies, if they cannot excel at global account management, they will likely be limited in their overall success to compete as a true global company.

In this chapter, we will explore what it takes to build the necessary competencies in business development systems, in particular, in the areas of global account management and its processes, along with the alliances necessary to successfully execute a global account management (GAM) program. This foundational pillar will help create a platform on which to successfully build and secure high, long-term, and sustainable global sales.

GLOBAL BUSINESS IS NOT JUST FOR THE FORTUNE 500 AND FINANCIAL TIMES (FT) 100

When we think of globalization, we tend to think of giants of business like the General Electric and the Nokias of the world as well as the rest of Fortune 500 in the United States and the Financial Times 100 (FT 100) in Europe. Who comes to mind are the industry leaders that we all know. We think of them because they have recognizable names and they have tremendous resources behind them to expand and impose their corporate presence virtually anywhere in the world. But that's changing and changing fast.

Today, a select cadre of small and midsize companies are going global, too. These enlightened nongiants are finding ways to exploit today's shortened product life cycles as well as ways to extend their reach on a global level. These small and midsize companies know how to deploy new information technology (IT) and telecommunications technologies and the Internet, and how to leverage key interdependencies with partner companies around the globe via carefully constructed strategic alliances and joint ventures. Such partnerships enable them to bring together much needed knowledge and resources to successfully exploit the tremendous opportunities that exist in distant markets around the world. These globally savvy companies are quickly learning to search beyond their own domestic markets to rich foreign markets and, especially, to key emerging markets that offer great potential for high growth rates and first-to-market opportunities that just can't be achieved at home.

As we fully explored in our earlier book, *Growing Your Business in Emerging Markets: Promise or Perils* (Quorum Publishing, 2000), notwithstanding the wild flurry of Internet-driven opportunities in the mid-1990s to the late 1990s, emerging markets represented *the* greatest new business opportunities for companies both large and small in the 1990s. But because small and midsize companies also faced tremendous resource challenges as they ventured overseas, they were collectively unable to capitalize on the vast opportunities in these markets to the same extent as the big guys were.

Today, however, going global means concentrating investments in IT and Internet infrastructure versus previous needed concentrations of expenditures in people and physical structures, which, by definition, yield lower productivity and returns on these investments. Today, for the first time, we are seeing a leveling of the playing field between large companies and their smaller competitors in the globalization of business as a direct result of IT and the Internet.

Ironically, as we stated in Chapter 1, it's the traditional mega-global companies that have paved the way and opened up so many of the doors in so many ways and in so many markets for the little guys to seriously play in the game of global business today. The time is now and the market is the world for companies of all sizes and in all industries to conduct *real* global business.

While the opportunities can be tremendous, going global also places heavy demands on the time of small and midsize company executives as they direct operations around the world and search for new opportunities in faraway places. Building global business requires new and specialized skills at all functional levels to deal with the various complexities and the diversities. And nowhere is it more important than to build key competencies and processes in the area of global account management.

GLOBAL ACCOUNT MANAGEMENT: WHY GLOBAL?

Global account management is simply the fully integrated sales and servicing of a strategically important business customer on a global basis. Although simply stated, it is one of the most challenging business development initiatives that any company can undertake. Its very existence is driven by the convergence of two inescapable trends: the globalization of business and the critical need to pursue business alliances for companies to succeed in business today.

Increasingly, a company's most strategically important customers are moving faster and faster into the global arena and attaining global company status themselves. Large and small suppliers alike, whether they are prepared for their own company globalization or not, are being forced to competently supply and service global customers or perish. To gain both the economies of scope (the ability to sell deep within and across a customer's organization worldwide) and the economies of scale (to effect cost efficiencies resulting from high-volume purchases and optimized operations), global customers are demanding that their suppliers are more proficient at selling, provisioning, and servicing their products to the customer's global business. Moreover, global customers are demanding comparable levels of pricing, on-time delivery, and customer and repair services from their suppliers on a worldwide basis. Leading global suppliers endeavor to provide effective and efficient global account management systems for their survival as well as to provide global transparency and high levels of customer service to their global customers' worldwide needs. The race is on!

GLOBAL ACCOUNT MANAGEMENT: ALLIANCES AT THE CORE

In a world of increasing alliances, to succeed in business at the global level, core competencies in creating alliances must be developed by *all* organizations. The new battle cry in global business today is, "Alliance or perish!" Any company with aspirations of growing beyond a domestic or regional market must do so to some extent through allying with other companies. Whether a company is a $100 billion-plus General Electric or a $100 million no-name company, it will need to form strategic business alliances with other companies and form them in varying degrees.

Developing the requisite core competencies to succeed in alliances is critical for any company hoping to get ahead in business today—domestically or globally. It is even more complex on the global business stage. Moreover, the need to develop alliances in *all* directions (see Figure 4.1) is demanded if any company, large or small, is to succeed, especially competing at a global business level. Companies that have attempted to go it alone and compete globally have systematically failed at almost every turn. The world is just too big, too diverse, and too complex for any company to tackle globalization on its own.

As one can see from the following examples, even very successful and sophisticated companies that believe they can globalize by operating essentially alone or by attempting any level of real alliancing without having the organizational competencies in place will be doomed to fail and jeopardize any globalization initiatives they may attempt.

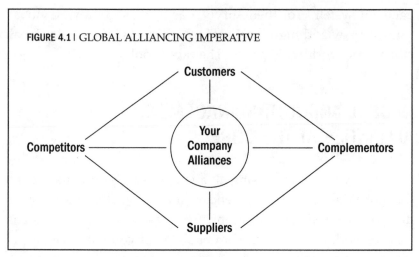

FIGURE 4.1 | GLOBAL ALLIANCING IMPERATIVE

Source: © Andrew-Ward International, Inc.

Alliancing *north* with customers, the "right" customers, i.e., those like-minded customers that value the strategic supplier alliance sought by the strategic supplier, is absolutely necessary. This alliancing serves as the basis for a supplier's global account management program, whether the customer is an end user of a major distributor or a reseller of a company's products or services.

Alliancing *south* with similarly like-minded suppliers is also required to successfully develop integrated supply chain management systems that enable a company to gain certain cost efficiencies as well as increased competitiveness within their markets, vis-à-vis, enhanced value propositions that can now be offered to customers resulting from such integrations.

Alliancing *east* with complementors enables companies to develop fully integrated product and service solutions to a common set of customers seeking a systems approach from its suppliers. All companies in all industries have potential complementors in their businesses. Complementors are simply third-party companies that add value to another company's products and services by offering their own different products and service in a combination that complements and makes the initial company's offering more valuable.

For example, the market leader in belt conveyor systems, Habasit S.A., headquartered in Bern, Switzerland, may partner with conveyor machine suppliers to provide a fully integrated "conveyance systems" solution approach to a common group of end-user textile or food manufacturing customers.

The most difficult and potentially problematic alliance development direction is *west*, i.e., alliancing with competitors, both directly and indirectly. John Caslione's company, Andrew-Ward International, Inc., has successfully constructed more than 200 national and strategic account management programs along with more than 60 global account management programs for companies with headquarters on four continents. Beginning in the early 1990s and continuing until today at an ever-increasing rate, the expanding globalization of business demands that competitors work more closely together in supplying and servicing common global customers. The days of ruthless competition that seek to "kill the competition" have given way to a new and enlightened notion that all companies can carry different labels at different times and with many companies simultaneously. For instance, while Mitsubishi supplies Motorola with high-tech components in one part of the company, Mitsubishi may also be a direct competitor as well as a complementor and a customer to Motorola, *all at the same time.*

A perfect example of two unlikely companies—and would-be competitors—joining forces to compete at a global level is the story of Metzler Optik Partner, a German-based optical frame manufacturer. For more than a decade Ulrich Fischer has dreamed of building his 170-year-old, privately held German optical frame-making business so it could compete with the industry's giants. "We want to become a top-tier player in the world," Fischer said. "For a company to become global, you need to achieve certain scale," continued Fischer, who is the chairman of the super-visory board of Metzler Optik Partner, which ranks number two in its German home market.[1]

Despite selling its products to about 70 major countries and cities around the world, largely through independent importers and distributors, Metzler is still well below the top-tier global players in size. "For a small entity, it is very difficult to compete with giant global corporations such as [global industry leader] Luxottica," Fischer said.[2]

His company has been looking for a strategic partner to help it achieve its global ambitions. Metzler portrayed itself as "a company seeking cooperation," shopping around for a partner. Fischer said it needed a partner that had localized distribution and sales networks and that knew local tastes.

Recently, the company forged a strategic alliance with Hong Kong–listed Moulin International Holdings. Moulin is an optical trading company that produces handmade frames for the local market and also makes and distributes branded frames such as Playboy, Giordano, Aigner, S.T. Dupont, and Elizabeth Arden.

The strategic alliance with Metzler will see the pair share resources and technologies to expand into the U.S. and Asian markets, by far the fastest growing regions in the world in this industry.

The two companies are effectively pooling resources as if they were a single entity, while at the same time remaining sep-arate companies in every other part of their businesses. By lever-aging the companies' production and sales network resources, both parties could quickly expand their business in the global market. Metzler uses Moulin's manufacturing facilities and dis-tribution network to develop mid-tier products for the U.S. mar-ket. Meanwhile, Metzler provides expertise on producing top-tier products and gives Moulin the guarantee of an original equipment manufacturer contract. Both fiercely independent and strong in their respective areas of the business, they are also very pragmatic and ambitious companies. While both seek to maintain their separate identities, each understands the need to leverage both strengths to build a powerful global business venture to compete against the global giants in their industry.

Companies—large and small—that understand this dynamic role shifting will have the greatest chance of success in the new global economy. When a strategically important global customer selects two directly competing suppliers to "handle *all* of that business customer's needs *worldwide*," and the customer essentially divides the business equally between these two suppliers and states, "I want you both to work together and make it all transparent to us," both suppliers must work closely together to deliver to the expectations of their common global customer. They must balance a close working relationship, while protecting proprietary and confidential company information—certainly not an easy task by any measurement. For anyone conducting business at this level, it has become more the rule than the exception to operate in this new dynamic, global alliance-driven mode.

GLOBAL ACCOUNT MANAGEMENT: FURTHER DEFINED

Like global organization, it is difficult to really pinpoint a precise definition for a global account management (GAM) program, or at least have a widespread consensus of what a definition may be. In any event, it is less important to create an exacting definition and more valuable to develop a list of attributes of a GAM program and how a successful GAM program should function. At a baseline level, a true GAM program consists of and exhibits the following key attributes:

- *Multicontinental* with full functional operations (e.g., manufacturing, sales, service, etc.) on a minimum of four continents

- Designed to provide *centralized account team responsibility and authority* (versus regional or national)

- Organized to enable *worldwide account team accountability*

- Designed to provide *dedicated, centralized and customized account servicing, billing, and administration*

- *Unequivocal commitment* from the supplier's executive management

- *Unrestricted active participation* from the supplier's executive management

Relatively speaking, however, few business customers and few suppliers today can actually perform global account management successfully. While many make carefully crafted, gallant attempts, many more make ill-conceived, misguided attempts and everything in between. Of the more than 600 national, strategic, and global account management programs that Andrew-Ward International has benchmarked in its research, more than 50 percent of these programs fail. The failure rate is the highest among those companies attempting global accounts management (almost 70 percent), when they have not taken the time to establish the proper internal global processes first, or they have chosen the wrong global account customer before launching a GAM program.

The basic demand for global account management generally is customer-driven. Typically, suppliers will not initiate such an ambitious undertaking without the suggestion first coming from one of their biggest customers. In those rare cases where a supplier actually initiates the idea of a GAM program with a targeted customer, the program can provide that supplier with a potentially tremendous competitive advantage as in the case of ABB Semiconductors, based in Lenzberg, Switzerland. This power semiconductor manufacturer will grow its business more than eightfold with a leading, global electric-drives manufacturer because it was the supplier, ABB, which initiated the global strategic supplier alliance program with this customer and literally taught the customer how to conduct business at a strategic level rather than merely at a price-oriented transactional level. ABB will accomplish all of this in under two years.

Under the visionary leadership of Stef Prina, ABB Semiconductor's director of sales, the company was able to establish a global strategic supplier alliance relationship in less than two years with this customer that will grow ABB's sales to this customer by more than 700 percent. Moreover, during the 18 months it took to accomplish this, Prina's team will have integrated key business processes with this global customer, enabling ABB to enjoy a sustainable strategic competitive advantage on a global basis far into the future.

At the heart of the failure of many global account management programs is the selection of the *wrong* global customer. An interesting and revealing trend has emerged that foretells whether the selection of a particular global account customer will, in fact, be a correct one. Global supplier programs that have been initiated by the global customer's procurement or purchasing department and then managed by that same department typically run into rough sailing and usually become problematic for the global supplier. Such initiations, it seems, are much too preoccupied with the global supplier's *price reductions* versus the more strategic and appropriate *cost reductions*. Yet, when such a global supplier's program has been initiated by the global customer's executive management and then managed by the global customer's procurement or purchasing management, the program has a far greater chance of succeeding. When the idea for such a program is initiated by executive management, then the global supplier program will have from its inception an inherently strategic focus to extend both the customer company's top-line global revenues and its overall competitiveness in the global arena along with its overall profitability. Oftentimes, under the initiation of most global procurement or purchasing departments, the program has, at its core, basically a global pricing discount program approach.

Our research has further revealed attributes that can be readily observed in both potential global customers as well as in potential global suppliers that will indicate to both parties the readiness and appropriateness of the other (and of themselves) to engage in such a high-stakes relationship. Potential global customers must be willing to:

- Make executive headquarter commitments to be a global company and have a comprehensive business plan to successfully achieve global status.

- Focus on one or two strategic global suppliers (to the extent possible) for each major category of their product or service needs globally.

- Accept "narrow-band" pricing versus an unrealistic single price for the same products and services from each supplier on a global basis.

- Take on responsibility for their share of daily procurement operations and administration with each supplier on a global basis (versus deferring to or "dumping" it on the global supplier).

Potential global suppliers must be willing to:

- Make executive headquarter commitments to be a global company and have a comprehensive business plan to successfully achieve global status.

- Consolidate centralized global account management responsibilities, authorities, and initiatives in the supplier's headquarter and enforce program compliance in the regions, individual markets, etc., globally.

- Prepare and execute a comprehensive plan to provide "narrow-band" pricing for the same products and services for each customer on a global basis.

- Prepare and execute a comprehensive customer service plan to provide consistent service levels for each customer on a global basis.

- Take on responsibility for their share of daily supply operations and administration with each customer on a global basis.

In the end analysis, both potential global customers and global suppliers considering undertaking any such program should remember that these programs are both difficult and complex, and even potentially dangerous to the business of both if not planned and executed properly. There must be compelling strategic reasons and/or significantly high volumes of business for both in the relationship. And while potentially high risks may be associated with implementing such programs, ready or not, the world economy is now primed and ready to provide a vast array of new opportunities to those companies willing to move forward boldly into the new global business arena.

Factors Correlating to Global Account Management Success

In the research conducted by Andrew-Ward International regarding the success profile of GAM programs, trends began to emerge as well as characteristics or factors that indicate what makes these programs successful. In fact, nine key factors seem to be evident in virtually all successful, well-established GAM programs that have been in operation for a minimum of three consecutive years. That is, the vast majority of successful GAM programs exhibited *all* these nine factors by their third full year of operation. Because this data was so compelling, a deeper analysis revealed that even if only one of the nine factors was not exhibited by a particular GAM program, then the probability of that program's success dropped by as much as 50 percent.

For practical purposes, it is rare, if not impossible, that any GAM program would immediately be launched with all nine factors in place and fully established. Virtually all of the programs analyzed slowly and over time began to adopt and internalize each of the nine factors that eventually correlated together and enabled GAM program success. The nine factors are:

1. Visible, tangible executive management commitment and support must exist.

2. All involved elements of the organization must be educated to the GAM program objectives and processes.

3. The company must develop measurable milestone activities to track the progress on each global account.

4. In the beginning, the GAM program must focus on only a few (one to three) high-profile targeted global accounts to conserve resources and establish and refine operational processes.

5. The global account manager must have the authority to commit the company.

6. Executive management must be available for crossover relationships with customers.

7. GAM communications must be separated from supplier's general business communications both for internal communications to its own organization and for external communications to the global account customer organization.

8. A primary GAM program objective is to penetrate the GAM customer's organization as high and as deep as

possible to cover the entire decision-making and operations level as possible.

9. The GAM team's compensation plan must not compete in any way with compensation plans for sales, service, distributor, and other support functions located in geographic regions, individual markets, or areas around the world.

The cost of failure is quite high. Imagine that a supplier makes all these assurances to a strategically important global customer that represents a tremendous amount of business for the supplier today and/or will in the future. Imagine that the customer relies on the supplier's assurances and begins to make a number of changes on a global basis to facilitate the two companies working together. These changes encompass things such as standardizing the customer's product and service needs to best comply and conform to the supplier's offerings, or integrating critical systems and process between the two companies. Then imagine the supplier failing to hold up its end of the deal. It probably would have been better if the supplier had not even initiated such a program in the first place.

What about the impact on an internal organization if this initiative fails? It is extremely difficult to restart a GAM program a second or a third time after it has failed the first time. Cynicism runs high and executive management will again be charged with more strategy du jour approaches to such new program initiatives.

Global Account Management Program Audit

The world—its businesses and its peoples—is moving quickly toward the inevitable economic integration of all humankind. The global economy will be with us forever; it is only a matter of to what extent or degree companies and individuals will be impacted by it, not whether there will be an impact. In the unforgiving and ruthless world of global business, companies both large and small need to develop as much positive momentum as possible in their global business strategies to succeed. A critical component of that global business plan is to properly launch a company's global account sales efforts with its targeted global account customers.

All companies, especially small and midsize companies whose limited resources place them immediately at a disadvantage with their larger competitors, will be greatly challenged in developing and executing successful global account management program. To assist these companies, we have included the Global Account Program Implementation Audit© (see Figure 4.2) from Andrew-Ward International's own implementation guidelines. In the audit that follows, companies will be able to assess their own company's readiness to take on the challenges of establishing a successful GAM program.

Answering the 12 questions in Figure 4.2 will provide an objective assessment of a company's ability to successfully implement a GAM program. The higher the number of "yes" answers recorded, the greater the likelihood a company will more easily and readily embrace and implement the requisite processes to establish a winning GAM program. Although there are some individual question-weighting considerations, typically a minimum of eight "yes" answers are needed for a company to build a viable GAM program that will be sustainable over five years or more. Below this minimum threshold, the probability of establishing a workable program drops to 50 percent or less, according to the research conducted by Andrew-Ward International.

For most companies, the difficult and painful transition from an organizational structure that is centered around its products or services, or its geographic markets (domestic and/or international regions), to a borderless market-driven and customer-focused organization is inevitable and unavoidable if the firm is to someday truly become a global company that succeeds in the high-stakes global marketplace. Readying and positioning the

FIGURE 4.2 | THE GLOBAL ACCOUNT MANAGEMENT PROGRAM
IMPLEMENTATION AUDIT

Top management support and involvement	Yes	No	Maybe
Executive availability for corporate-to-corporate relationship building	Yes	No	Maybe
IT and IS capability for global account tracking and communication	Yes	No	Maybe
A willingness and ability to administer target accounts from a centrally controlled corporate HQ program	Yes	No	Maybe
A willingness and ability to administer pricing from a centrally controlled HQ program	Yes	No	Maybe
A willingness and ability to restructure volume and profit accountability from local organizations or subsidiaries to corporate HQ —Credit issues —Compensation issues	Yes	No	Maybe
A willingness and ability to "impose" negotiated GAM account requirements on country operations, subsidiaries, or local distribution	Yes	No	Maybe
Current multicontinental operations capability: —All operations meet global standards and certification requirements for your industry (e.g., ISO 900X, CE, regulatory)	Yes	No	Maybe
Ability to design and deliver (1) standard; (2) custom product or service solutions from all global operation locations	Yes	No	Maybe
A willingness and ability to manage global finance, billing, collections, credit, etc., from a centrally controlled HQ program, if required	Yes	No	Maybe
Ability to control and manage production and logistics requirements from a centrally controlled HQ program	Yes	No	Maybe
A willingness and ability to provide standardized service, support, and training from any operations unit, in local language and respecting local culture and customs	Yes	No	Maybe

Source: Andrew-Ward International, Inc.

company to succeed in global account management is certainly one of the most critical components of any successful company formula. The Global Account Program Implementation Audit© (Figure 4.2), albeit simple, clear, and direct, is only the first step that must be taken by an aspiring global company if it intends to develop, execute, and sustain a viable and effective GAM program.

GAM Program and the Need for Strategic Business Alliances

For most small and midsize companies, the very thought of assembling a global account management team may be so over-whelming that it can prevent a company from even attempting such a program. To think that a $100 million to $500 million com-pany can put together a credible internal GAM team in as many as 40 or 50 markets on as many as four continents may be a hal-lucination to some. And it may very well be if this small or mid-size company intends to go it alone. Because it is a world of business alliances, companies of virtually any size must seriously consider how to extend business alliance philosophies to their GAM programs as well.

Take the case of SPL, part of the Dimension Data Group. SPL has long been recognized as a high-value IT partner to South African corporations and to government. The company focuses on customer management, information management, and enter-prise systems. Over the past decade or so, SPL invested heavily to position itself as the dominant player in providing total cus-tomer relationship management (CRM) solutions in South Africa. As part of this drive, the company forged a strategic partnership with Siebel Enterprise Systems based in the United States. Siebel Systems is a market leader in enterprise-class sales, marketing, and customer-service information systems focused on increasing sales and service effectiveness.

Companies like SPL that recognize the tremendous opportunities that await them in the new global marketplace realize that they need to position themselves differently if they have any chance of becoming a real global player. One way to begin is to change their thinking and make far-reaching changes to their traditional sales strategies and business processes.

"These changes will inevitably be challenging," believes Johann Coetzee, general manager at SPL, "but the ability to manage customer relationships on a worldwide basis is already proving to be a key competitive differentiator."[3]

As customer expectations rise, companies that can provide better service globally will retain a competitive advantage. What is key to successful global selling is the formation of global account management relationships.

"To sell throughout the world, organizations need to establish true global account relationships with key customers, and use technology as the cornerstone to implement these changes," says Coetzee. "Traditional methods of relationship selling and management cannot scale to meet the needs of organizations doing business in multiple countries, multiple currencies, and multiple business conditions."[4]

Until now, U.S.- or UK-based companies have awarded global customer status to certain key customers, and several South African subsidiaries of international companies are global customers by virtue of these agreements. Today, many major South African companies, having lagged behind, are now poised to establish true global selling relationships with their key multinational accounts.

Those companies who are going this route are reaping the rewards on a global scale—and these rewards are big. The companies are finding current as well as new customers sending more business their way in exchange for the special treatment the customers receive as global accounts with all the special advantages that such status brings, e.g., guaranteeing a superior level of service worldwide; ensuring lower total cost of ownership; priority access to new innovative products, services technologies, process improvements, etc., on a global basis.

To set up such global account relationships with key customers, however, companies need to reengineer their sales practices to keep up with global market changes. True global account management requires a refinement of the strategies and process improvements already in place. Such an approach is much less a sales program and more of a management program made up of a series of business development, process improvement, and systems integration projects.

The strategic changes necessary to the global account strategy must also include an expanded view of profitability. Profit sacrifices may be necessary in one region or market for increased global profitability, for example. Regional profit centers have to become global in outlook.

"This change is among the most difficult aspects of implementing global sales processes and strategies," says Coetzee. "Sales force incentives have to be adapted to the goal of nurturing global accounts that are likely to bring profitable volume sales."[5]

It is also vital that companies invest in the right customers and are selective about whom they award global status. They need to do this to ensure that over the long term they can create opportunities for increased customer share.

Also vital to successful global selling is the right technological infrastructure. "Sales, marketing, and customer service automation can play a key role in expanding an enterprise's ability to manage global customer relationships," says Coetzee, who adds that the new U.S. leader in enterprise relationship management systems, Siebel, provides a solution that embraces all these key elements.

"By allowing organizations to share information across the global enterprise, they can deliver products and services that meet customer requirements regardless of international boundaries," adds Coetzee.[6]

As SPL and Siebel have clearly shown, by alliancing in new creative ways, and coupling advanced information technology, their joint, now global, enterprise can provide an enhanced level of services to global account customers that could never be possible if either company would have attempted to go it alone. Moreover, these two companies, one known as a market leader in the United States and the other barely known beyond its domestic market, have joined together to provide an expanded presence that will enable them to both collectively compete and succeed on a global level even against some of the biggest global companies around.

SUMMARY

As we have examined the activities of a handful of small and midsize companies that have been able to successfully transition from domestic-bound to global, we have come to see that their successes in global account management helped enable them to make the needed transition. From ABB Semiconductors to Metzler Optik to SPL, each company achieved successes they could not have achieved if they had acted alone. In fact, most of them would have had very little chance to break out of their domestic business development models if it hadn't been for some enlightened leadership with a vision of their companies' global future along with a healthy measure of some astute risk taking.

The critical importance of carefully planning and executing a global strategy cannot be overstated. As AOL's chief executive officer Steve Case puts it, "In the end, a vision without the ability to execute is probably a hallucination."[7] Simply stated, without the successful implementation of programs like global account management to serve as key strategic execution vehicles, any visions of global business that may be articulated by any CEO have relatively little value beyond the short-term hype and chaotic activity it may create.

The fate of global companies, whether global customers or global suppliers, lies in the hand of the other. Both have tremendous opportunities that lie ahead of them on the new global landscape. They equally take tremendous risk, with consequences that await them if either of them gets it wrong. Never before has the world of business so much relied on the need for strategic business alliances of companies to achieve a common and collective goal—the goal of capturing new, untapped business that exists in the new, interdependent global marketplace. And as global buyers and global sellers get swept up in the fury and the frenzy of the new global marketplace, competition and risk of failure increase exponentially. Both need to get it right and get it right together.

Global account management represents an opportunity for both global customers and suppliers today, or those aspiring to become global tomorrow, to exploit the promise of the new global economy as well as mitigate the perils it also holds. While the desire to succeed may be great and the ideas clear, a successful GAM program is, at best, complex and politically charged, time-consuming, and simply very tricky to execute. These programs have a failure rate that exceeds 50 percent, and when they fail, they fail a miserable death, leaving relationships shattered and businesses destroyed.[8]

Most traditional buyer and seller partnership programs in the past have been little more than convenient vehicles for snappy slogans and tired clichés eventually leading to just more adversarial finger-pointing when the joint business initiative runs into rough sailing. Competing at the global level with all its inherent land mines to knock companies offtrack makes it that much more important that customers and suppliers work even harder and more closely with an eye to guarantee their common business success in what could aptly be called a spirit of global "mutual self-interest."

CHAPTER 5

GLOBAL CUSTOMER SERVICE

As global manifest destiny continues to expand and economically integrate more of the world's population, the battle to find and keep good customers is becoming increasingly ferocious. New tactics and new strategies are needed to ward off the attackers.

The days are long gone when a company can rest on its laurels with the assurance that its customers will not stray to "the other side." Moreover, if you've spent a lot of money and resources working to obtain your customers, don't risk losing them to poor customer service. Inventory shortages, back orders, and long delivery times can quickly eat up your profits with returns and canceled orders. This has been true for some time now, whether a company is only doing business domestically or starting to venture into the new global marketplace. The challenges are certainly compounded, sometimes exponentially, when dealing at the global level.

To maintain and grow relationships with existing customers or to initiate business with new ones, companies are compelled to constantly and consistently provide the best products at competitive prices and at the highest levels of service possible. Only now, companies must find ways to do all this on a global level.

As a result of this new decree from the global marketplace, companies need to focus on providing the best service to their customers. But that's a problem. Every company, in every industry, wants to deliver quality customer service. Therefore, the real question before global business leaders is *not* "How do I offer and deliver stronger customer service?" Instead, the fundamental questions are: "How do I develop a global customer service strategy?" and "What must I actually do to deliver high-quality customer service globally?"

DEVELOPING A GLOBAL CUSTOMER SERVICE STRATEGY

For most companies doing global business, the only thing their customers share is probably the fact that they buy the same products and services. However, beyond basic product requirements, global customers are as unique as the culture and nation from which they come. In addition, global customers can differ in terms of product application, geographic area, market mix, and target markets.

A successful global customer service strategy must recognize customers' differences and then address these differences as fundamental parts of the global customer service strategy. This is best accomplished by:

- *Customer focus.* Learn what is most important to your customers.

- *Overdelivery.* Exceed customer expectations.

- *Flexibility.* Respond quickly and appropriately.

- *Adaptability.* Growth requires the continuous ability to embrace change.

- *Value.* Differentiate your company's offerings in a commoditized world.

- *Empathy.* Get into the customer's thinking.

- *Spotting trends.* Listen for the future.

- *Reinforcing your message.* Remind customers about *you.*

Customer Focus

Global customer service should be far more than a department title or a promotional slogan; it should be an integral part of the global strategic plan. Partnering with your key suppliers to deliver recognized and measurable global customer service should be as much a part of the corporate culture as achieving sales goals, increasing inventory turns, or improving return on investment.

The proper execution of a global customer strategy must clearly address the expectations and needs of a company's key customers. To best do this, many global firms learn as much as they can about the top 20 percent of their customers, who probably represent about 80 percent of their business (Pareto's Rule of 80/20). Some of the ways this is done include:

- Hold regular meetings with a key customer's functional management groups.

- Meet routinely with key distribution partners in each market where your company employs independent distributors or agents to market, sell, or service your company's products and services.

- Conduct local market customer focus groups for the smaller customers (nonglobal account customers) and consumers, whenever necessary.

- Engage in discussions with end users of your company's products and services.

- Observe first-hand selected customers' business and work processes and procedures in selected key markets (or all of their individual markets if necessary), especially as they relate to how customers use your products or services.

- Document each key customer's, customer segment's, or industry segment's unique traits and capabilities by individual market.

- Share all relevant information with your company's own sales, marketing, manufacturing, and customer service personnel, which will help to enhance customer service globally and locally.

Overdelivery

Implementing successful global customer service requires carefully analyzing customers individually, the major customer groups and in specific markets, to find specific areas where a company can excel in terms of product and service offerings and the accompanying customer service. The ultimate objective is to consistently exceed the customer's expectations. Some of the ways this can be accomplished include:

- Make it easy for customers to do business with you.

- Develop your own Web site and pursue e-commerce for product information, order entry, project status, and so forth.

- Demand accurate and reliable shipping dates from your vendors and handle field installation and quality issues in a priority manner.

- Keep your customers apprised of current codes and regulations and share new product information from your key suppliers.

Flexibility

The ability to be flexible and change quickly is fundamental to global business success. The great distances and dimensions that affect the normal conduct of global business implore leaders to maintain a high degree of flexibility. In addition to the routine global customer service issues, things can get off track really fast and in a big way when you elevate business to a multi-continental level—perhaps due to weather, material supply problems, or myriad other reasons, and with little or no warning.

To constantly improve their level of global customer service, leaders align themselves with manufacturers and other suppliers who are also flexible. They also develop delivery programs unilaterally or with their suppliers that use their own warehouse facilities as a resource to always be best positioned to meet their global customers' service requirements.

Adaptability

In global markets, customer groups and market segments will most likely differ in terms of product and service requirements from one market to another in each newly entered market. As with any new experience, bringing new product and service offerings will require adaptation to each local market's needs and wants, especially as experience in these markets grows and evolves.

Not only will your company's product and service offerings need to be adapted to each local market over time, but also the customer service organization will have to adapt to changes in each market. Very often, the company will assemble specific groups within the customer service organization that will become market or regional experts. These groups will ensure that the proper level of localization and regionalization is brought to bear on each appropriate market and region to provision high-quality market- and culturally sensitive customer service.

Unlike adapting to changes in a domestic market, global customer service organizations will need either to develop their own internal expertise or develop trusted alliances with local distributors or agents, their marketing and sales people, and local market research firms. Customer and consumer information and competitive product and service information are essential for the successful global company to identify trends in faraway markets, so the company can be competitive and maintain and enhance its customer service.

Value

It is oftentimes said that value is total benefits delivered minus price. If price is the only measurement for products and services, then there usually is no differentiating value to the buyer in today's world of commoditized products and services. If there is no perceived value, product and service become a commodity, and there is no measurable way to differentiate one supplier from another.

To ensure value, global firms must partner to provide clear, consistent, and reliable product and service features that deliver measurable benefits to customers and end users. A few obvious—and often overlooked—traits of extraordinary customer service include: quality products, complete and on-time deliveries; unexpected product and service features at no extra cost, professional and knowledgeable support staff, problem solving, and attention to detail.

Empathy

Global firms consider what they want from manufacturing partners—certainly more than a competitive price point. They want reliability, effective promotions, market intelligence, specification interpretation, loyalty, unique sales features, and polite and courteous personal attention. This list is basic, but it is *not* negotiable. All items must be present all the time to ensure satisfaction. A global customer service strategy makes sure a firm is giving its customers the same consideration.

Spotting Trends

Global firms continually ask their customers what they want and what they expect. They try to spot trends before their competitors, and they carefully listen for subtle ways to improve their customer service. They also search for what their competitor is doing well, not doing, or doing poorly. Moreover, besides the salesperson selling the actual product or service, it is the customer service person who has ongoing contact and communication with customers and consumers using the product or service. In fact, even more than the salesperson, it is the customer service representative whose primary responsibility it is to service the customer and who is in a better position to probe customers and consumers in a nonthreatening manner (i.e., servicing versus selling).

As the founder of Sony was once quoted as saying when he spotted a new emerging trend: "We do not create products, we create markets." His new company's initial success was launched with the development of the Sony Walkman, which capitalized on the trend he saw that the emerging baby-boom generation embraced music as a new "religion." So it is that a global company's customer service organization will need to work very closely with global marketing, sales, and product and service development groups to communicate new trend information it receives from customers. The global customer service organization also serves a vital role as a key conduit for these departments to elicit perceptions, opinions, experiences, and other needed information from customers and consumers. With such invaluable information, the global company is in the best position to spot and confirm trends, and then to capitalize on them with new and enhanced product and service offerings.

Reinforcing Your Message

How customers view their suppliers may be directly related to how often they are reminded of how they are being supported. Global firms let their customers know what is done for them on a regular basis, both in terms of products delivered and customer service support.

To help you go further in delivering excellent customer service to customers globally, here are a few key areas on which to focus.

Make ordering easy. Superior global customer service starts from the first customer contact. Make it especially easy for your customers to order from you and in as many different ways as suits their own needs. Spend time adapting your company's ordering processes right down to the forms you ask customers to fill out. Pay close attention to the following:

- *Customer name and address.* Make sure you leave plenty of space for the name and address; foreign addresses tend to be a lot longer than U.S. addresses.

- *Instructions.* If you are selling clothing or shoes, reduce the number of potential customer returns by providing easy access to easy-to-read size conversions. By adapting your product and service descriptions and order form into the local language and preferred color schemes, you also will reduce any possible confusion by the customer when they are ordering from you.

- *Mailings.* If you are mailing anything directly to the customer in English, consider a multilingual format with ordering instructions in both English and all local languages. Also, be sure to specify that the customer complete the information in printed Roman characters. If you don't, you may need to have your orders deciphered or translated. This will take a lot more time than you think and cost more.

- *Customer responses.* Provide your customers with alternative and convenient ways to respond to you: telephone, fax, mail, or Web. Most orders taken today in the United States still are done by telephone. This is not necessarily the case in other markets where the cost of a telephone call is much higher, and most orders are placed via fax or through the mail. If you are selling business to business, you need to include an Internet option as well as a fax option. Despite the seemingly ubiquitous use of the Internet, many business-to-business orders are still received via fax.

Handling customer orders. If your company offers a telephone ordering option, carefully consider how you will handle incoming calls from customers in foreign markets. How will your company route these calls to its domestic operation? Will your company set up facilities in Europe or Asia? Differing cultures, multiple languages, time, and operating costs are key reasons why it often makes sense to set up an overseas call center. Although many people living outside of North America comprehend and speak English to varying degrees, they typically feel more comfortable talking in their native language when placing orders and requesting service.

A foreign-based customer call center may make financial sense, too. It is generally less costly to have a large volume of calls that originate in Europe also terminate in Europe at a European customer call center. Also, if foreign calls are being routed to a U.S.-based call center, make sure your company considers time zone changes when it schedules its customer call center hours.

Be sure your company understands the preferred methods of payment in each local market and then offer a variety of market-appropriate payment options. The United States and Canada are still largely check-based economies, whereas most of the rest of the world (industrialized or developing markets) are transaction-based economies that use either direct debit or bank transfer. Also, cash on delivery, check, or payment by invoice may be other options to be considered.

Unlike the United States and Canada, it would be a mistake to assume that customers will pay by credit card. In much of Europe and especially in Germany, the payment for most mail-order goods is done on open account; that is, customers are billed only after the product is received and received in good order.

Product fulfillment. Product fulfillment depends on the products your company is shipping, the company's acceptable turnaround time, and its investment in global markets, including global customer service. If your company is in the early stages of developing its global business or if it has products with relatively low rates of return, it should generally consider using its current domestic fulfillment operation. If your company's strategy is committed to establishing a fully globalized business or it has products that have high rates of return, it may be better to set up foreign product fulfillment operations or hire a local market firm to handle local order fulfillment.

How your company ships products will impact delivery time. It will be a lot cheaper to ship products via ocean freight, but your company will definitely save more time by sending products by airfreight.

Also, if you are shipping products as individual orders using the U.S. Postal Service (USPS), or your company's freight consolidator uses the USPS as its delivery agent, the order travels as mail from your company to the customer. This can be quite expensive. Alternatively, if the package is being shipped from the United States for delivery by a foreign postal administration, the package travels to the destination country as cargo and then becomes mail on entering the postal system of the destination country—typically at lower cost to your company.

If your company is distributing from a foreign fulfillment location, products usually leave the United States in bulk. Then the products are delivered to your company's overseas operation or a contracted operation in the local market. The local fulfillment operation then separates the merchandise and packages and addresses the orders. Packages enter the local market postal distribution system via an optimized and cost-effective fulfillment scheme.

Customer returns and refunds. To provide superior customer service, companies should not allow currency fluctuations to impact a customer's refund. Customers around the world should be reimbursed at the same conversion rate as when the sale was processed. Companies and customers should not seek to make or lose money on returns or refunds.

Decisions to reimburse customers for postage spent to return an item usually depend on your company's profit margin on that product or that specific order or order type. If margins are substantial, companies may want to refund the customer for any shipping costs incurred to demonstrate their dedication to superior customer service and to motivate the customer for future purchases.

CREATING GLOBAL CUSTOMER SERVICE STANDARDS

When creating standards for global customer service, global firms make certain that they are measurable. For example, one objective may be 100 percent packing accuracy. Perfect packing inspection is not an objective; it is one possible solution. Packing inspection is only one task of many that could achieve the objective. Other tasks or alternatives may be more effective for accomplishing the objective.

How will you measure the objective on an ongoing basis? If you cannot measure an objective, you will never know whether it was achieved. For example, 100 percent shipping accuracy may be measured using statistical sampling after final packing but prior to shipment.

Establish Global Customer Service Rules and Constraints

Identify key restrictions (hard rules) and guidelines (soft rules) that will form the boundaries of your customer service strategy. These rules include company policies, expected return on investment, project organization, personnel availability, computer system development/support constraints, and internal operations procedures.

The rules represent key compromises between revenue producers (customer support, marketing, and sales personnel) with operations, engineering, MIS, and other project resources. Only upper management can change the rules and guidelines after the project starts. These rules are the foundation for effective communication and timely decision making.

Disassemble Each Objective into Unique Tasks

A task identifies what must be accomplished, not how. After analyzing the objectives, clearly identify what tasks are within the scope of the global customer service team and prioritize the tasks to optimize dependencies and return on investment. The task definition and sequence are very critical to the effectiveness of the program.

It is important to establish minimum customer service standards, make sure everyone understands them, and have a way to recognize superior performance. As procedures are developed, make sure all three criteria are satisfied. Use creative problem-solving techniques to develop a list of feasible solutions for the task. Select a combination of possible solutions that will accomplish the objective with minimal ongoing effort.

MAINTAINING GLOBAL CUSTOMER SERVICE STANDARDS

Beyond developing a global customer service strategy, a global firm must maintain customer service standards for their employees, suppliers, and, ultimately, their customers. Unfortunately, some companies have not understood the need to enhance their customer service functions and create standards, because they assumed it was not required or the benefits were not tangible. Historically, it has been wiser to wait until external circumstances (e.g., economic conditions, product trends) warranted some change. Such thinking is clearly contradictory to the proactive global customer service approach demanded if a company is to transform itself into a truly successful global company competing in the new global marketplace.

What Are the Standards We Are Maintaining?

Maintaining standards may involve the weekly or monthly analysis of the measurement of a company's global customer service standards. Such questions as Can we offer additional services that the customer may not be aware we offer? or What would it take to have the customer use only our services? make this process more fluid and responsive to customer needs.

Handling Complaints

Companies must maintain standards for the handling of complaints. One study by the Technical Assistance Research Program Institute shows 70 percent of unhappy global customers will not make another purchase from an offending firm. On the other hand, 95 percent of customers will return if their complaint is resolved quickly. It goes without saying that effective, speedy resolution of complaints keeps customers happy.

SUMMARY

Successful global customer service doesn't just happen; it must be planned, implemented, monitored, and continually refined. The creation of a global customer service strategy and the organization to deliver it successfully require developing and fine-tuning new management processes to bring about exceptional customer service on a global scale. Shifting an organization's central focus from primarily domestic customers to customers in markets in the four corners of the world means that extraordinary multicultural customer relations and service need to become a natural operating procedure. When customers from markets around the world feel that they are the central and primary concern of a company, they buy more and repeatedly from that company, regardless of where that company may be located, whether around the corner or around the world.

Making the shift from a domestically focused customer service approach to a global customer service approach requires a complete change of mindset of how a company does business. Such new thinking will undoubtedly require customer service executives to concentrate on the critical success factors of people, process, technology, and environment—and all of these at a global level. Ultimately, a tight focus on these critical factors leads to the creation of an environment that supports the acquisition and maintenance of the right people, the right processes, and the right technology to compete on a global basis.

Moreover, a true, sustainable competitive advantage will be built through long-term dedication to developing a full global customer service strategy and, more important, by evolving such a strategy when implemented as a comprehensive approach to building the total global company in the exploding borderless economy.

CHAPTER 6

GLOBAL E-BUSINESS

Until the tech crash that began in March 2000, there was no lack of dot-com obsession. Everyday we were inundated with information from experts who told us e-business will revolutionize the way business gets done. The future's promised land of the Internet, supposedly, was all that mattered.

Conventional wisdom began to view bricks-and-mortar companies as dinosaurs on the brink of extinction. Arguments in the hallowed halls of some of America's finest business schools concluded that there was almost no way a traditional business could survive in the face of e-commerce without dramatically altering its business model. The dot-coms, many believed, were creating the new business models for winning and keeping loyal customers. To confirm all this, Jeff Bezos, the founder of Amazon.com, was named *Time* magazine's Man of the Year in 1999. The old economy, it seemed, was being guillotined and e-business was the blade.

Despite the plummet in share values, there is some justification to this belief. Consumer spending online is approaching $100 billion worldwide per year. A large cross section of consumers report they prefer shopping online over the more conventional methods. And the number of companies and consumers buying online is rising logarithmically every year.

According to Forrester Research, the premier high-tech consultancy, global e-business is about to reach a threshold from which it will accelerate into hypergrowth. Intercompany trading of goods over the Internet, Forrester conservatively projects, will double every year until 2005, surging from $43 billion the past year to $1.3 trillion in 2003. If the value of services exchanged or booked online were included as well, the figures would be even more staggering.

In the face of these numbers, companies are investing millions, and even billions of dollars, in e-business to capture market share and build customer loyalty.

News of most of these investments seems to be dominated either by companies in the Global 500 or those Internet start-ups that emerged as the titans of the new economy in the late 1990s. Companies from the venerable Nestlé headquartered in bucolic Vevey, Switzerland, that plans to invest as much as $1.8 billion over a period of three years to become one of the world's Web-smart elite,[1] to Silicon Valley's Cisco Systems, a company whose name is synonymous with Internet architecture, are two such companies. Countless other companies of all sizes spent several thousands to several millions of dollars and more on new information technologies during these ramp-up years.

Such ubiquitous integration of new IT has given rise to new opportunities for businesses all over the world—large companies and not-so-large-companies, new and old companies alike.

The Internet and its attendant power have made it possible for many companies to conduct global business at a much more discernible and attainable level. New economies and efficiencies of scale have been created. Not too long ago, only a few companies had the resources to compete on a global scale. Now, more than at any time in history, almost any size firm with the vision and ambition to do so can extend its reach globally.

As a result of the Internet and new information technology, many of the myths about globalization can be unmasked. According to one theory, globalization is a conspiracy by big companies against smaller markets. Some companies, of course, are bigger, financially, than others. That's a testimony to the market-based economy that more and more markets are choosing to adopt. But no company or group of companies is calling all the shots. Small and midsize companies are getting in on the act and thriving globally.

Because of the Internet and its impact on global business, entirely new companies and business models are emerging in industries ranging from chemicals to road transport and are bringing together buyers and sellers in superefficient new electronic marketplaces. All this gives many managers a terrible sense of déjà vu. They have been through outsourcing, downsizing, and reengineering. They may well have undergone the frequently nightmarish experience of putting in the packaged IT applications that automate internal processes and manage supply chains, and may still be wondering whether it was worth spending all those millions of dollars. Nearly all of them embraced the low cost and flexibility of PC-based so-called client/server computing at the start of the 1990s, only to discover the perils of decentralizing data and distributing complexity. And, more recently, they invested lots of time and money into nothing more exciting than avoiding a system's meltdown on the first day of the new millennium.

No wonder many of them are asking themselves whether e-business is a friend or a foe. Whether it presents the most exciting opportunities in a generation or the most terrifying challenges they have ever faced seems unclear. Yet, most of them know that the Internet is entirely different from the technology-driven changes they have either embraced or had thrust on them in the past. Most leaders realize that most previous IT investments have focused internally, concentrating on making each business more efficient.

By contrast, the Internet is all about communicating, connecting, and transacting with the outside world—the new globally interconnected world and the new global economy—regardless of the size of the company or the company's founding. Its benefits derive not just from speeding up and automating a company's own internal processes, but from spreading the efficiency gains to the business systems of its suppliers and customers of all sizes, in all markets.

Certainly technology matters, but getting the business strategy right matters even more. And that may mean not just reengineering a company, but giving it a new birth. This new birth is a metamorphosis from an essentially domestically focused company to a company focused on the entire world—a true global company.

WHAT IS GLOBAL E-BUSINESS?

Global e-business is not a simple undertaking. It involves a variety of complex issues. Moreover, failure to adequately address the IT element can alienate entire markets and erode the relationship between a company and the marketplace. A comprehensive global e-business strategy can greatly help to ensure a place in the global economy, thus enabling a business to take advantage of a world of possibilities.

Global e-business strategically uses IT to take apart physical supply chains and reassemble them in better ways, create highly focused communications for specific cultures, and select the parameters needed to support multiple markets.

Global e-business adapts specific IT to a company's products and message to best meet the varied expectations of markets around the world. In addition, global e-business is, in many ways, a complete revolution of how a company perceives distance, time, and location.

Global e-business is the most powerful communications medium the business world has ever known, in large part because of its reach into factories, offices, and homes around the world. The substantially lower cost of communication via the Internet has dramatically lessened the importance of distance. For many products that can be digitized—such as pictures, video, sound, and words—distance will become a nonfactor. The same is true for services. And even for most products, because of the Internet, distance will have much less an effect on overall business costs.

In the physical world, time and season predominate the flow of goods and services around the world. We see this in the hours of operation—activities that occur by time of day and in social and climactic seasons. The virtual marketplace, on the other hand, is always open. The seller need not be awake, or even physically present, for the buyer to be served by the seller. The Internet is independent of season. Time can thus be homogenized—made uniformly consistent for all buyers and for all sellers.

Because any screen-based activity can be operated anywhere on earth, location does not play an important part in most business decisions. Is it even relevant? Does location mean where the firm is officially registered? Is it where most of the people employed by the company work? Or is it where the server is physically located? In most cases, it simply doesn't matter.

Following the recent decade's IT explosion, a world marketplace awaits, with its entire attendant of consumers and competition. An initial presence on the Internet can be relatively easy and inexpensive to establish. And any company that has a presence on the World Wide Web is international by definition, whether it chooses to become a global company or not.

Global e-business exploits the Internet's ability to level the playing field for all participants, regardless of size, especially as it relates to a company's ability to communicate with customers, employers, suppliers, investors, and other targeted groups. No other media can claim this ability. No individual or company has a better right to establish a place on the Web than any other. Mere purchasing of limited physical space in newspapers or magazines, or buying time on radio or TV, cannot achieve such presence. No other medium can even come close to achieving the level of scalability that the Internet can achieve, i.e., the ability to leverage its own power and impact to much higher levels and with a much broader global reach.

Global e-business eliminates the historic rigid hierarchy of business processes. According to leading corporate strategists, individual workers must be given maximum autonomy, and the patterns of communications within a worldwide organization should resemble a knowledge-based ecology more than a flowchart. All of this is irrespective of a company's size and physical location.

The challenge for businesses of all sizes—especially smaller ones—that want to maximize their global presence involves structuring relationships and information flow so that the right parties can obtain the information at the right time. In all these views, IT and e-business initiatives play critical roles in the strategy of global competition, especially in regard to their global supply chain application.

Global e-business is absolutely a critical component in managing the global supply chain. It is one area of business that can benefit the most from new processes enabled by e-business technologies. If companies are not ready for this next century, they could easily become panicked, whether the company is large or small. For example, the interval between the time when products leave a manufacturer's site in Taiwan and when they arrive on the company's receiving dock in France is often an informational black hole. Companies may not know if there's a problem with goods delayed in customs, bad weather in Asia or anywhere along the route, or just slow shipments from the regional warehouses caused by another truckers' strike outside of Paris. In fact, there may be no problem at all; but they'll never know from their internal reports.

Companies that know how to leverage global e-business strategies into Internet-enabled global supply chain management systems no longer see themselves as standing alone or out of touch. Instead, these savvy companies focus on their role as part of a supply chain, with a web of integrated links to customers, suppliers, and other business partners. This approach requires a shift in focus from an internal or product perspective to a pure customer-centric, business partner–oriented mind-set.

Before the advent of the new information and e-business technologies of the past decade and before easy access to global information systems became available to companies, customers and suppliers had to make major decisions with little information on which to base them. With the global e-business solutions, buyers and suppliers of all sizes can now easily track the status and current location of their orders around the world. Before this proliferation of global e-business capability was available, small and midsize companies, especially, might have found themselves left out of the countless new business opportunities in an exploding global economy.

Obviously, small and midsize companies do not possess the sizable resources usually reserved for the biggest global companies in the world. At the same time, those that will succeed in the future understand that the Internet and e-business technology are invaluable, indispensable business tools that need to be harnessed and crafted into a company's overall strategies. To ensure success on the new global business frontier, business leaders from these companies must do what they've always had to do: formulate and implement ideas, tactics, and strategies. Now, they must do this at a much higher level—at a global level—to enable their companies to survive and prosper in the new global marketplace.

DEVELOPING YOUR GLOBAL E-BUSINESS STRATEGY

The greatest challenge for all businesses that want to truly maximize their global presence centers on structuring relationships and the flow of information so that the right parties—customers, suppliers, employees, etc.—can obtain it at the right time and at the right place. In this view, e-business and IT initiatives play critical roles in forging a successful global company. This is especially true for small and midsize businesses.

Many companies, however, large and small, wrongly believe e-business and IT will harvest big rewards by merely overlaying computers on top of traditional work processes. These companies fail to understand that e-business and IT work best when they are used to transform those same traditional processes as well as the entire corporate culture. The most successful companies specifically focus on ways that e-business and IT can add value to existing business systems by gaining improved and increased efficiencies. Such a mind-set and resulting strategy affords a small and midsize company the ability to develop entirely new business capabilities and processes to then forge the company's global presence.

Globally savvy companies and their managers view projects, as well as the business overall, from a global perspective. Striving to overcome cultural challenges, regional, national, and personal differences are subrogated to the overall global good of the company to maximize results for the entire organization. Leaders of these companies realize that success depends on the unrestricted flow of information throughout their global business network, which then comes together in the right place and at the right time. For these companies, this doesn't happen by chance. It's a function of its global company culture, and at its core, it is this culture that drives the global organization and, in turn, its global business success. Now, more than ever, e-business technology is driving culture and this new culture is driving globalization.

E-business Strategy: Manifestly Global

The new digital economy is manifestly global—a global phenomenon, yet truly globalized e-businesses are the exception. Even the largest companies on the planet still have a ways to go before they can claim total globalization. Globalization of a company's e-business processes or its Internet presence is not a simple task. It engages a variety of complex issues, and language translation is just the beginning. Failure to sufficiently tackle e-business globalization can isolate entire markets and jeopardize relationships between a company and the marketplace. Moreover, it has the potential to erode and destroy a company's business on a regional or global scale. A cogent and inclusive e-business globalization strategy can ensure a company's place in the new borderless digital economy, enabling businesses of all sizes to exploit a new world of opportunities.

A global marketplace awaits all business, with all the attendant customers, consumers, competition, and suppliers that this entails. This is an exciting time for business, indeed, but also a potentially dangerous time. Companies of all sizes too often are blinded by the promises of the new global economy. Herein lays the seductive danger of the Internet and its creation of e-business. Harvesting the Internet's potential rewards requires more than just making a company Internet-enabled. Companies that want to offer their products and services to the world and successfully compete in the new global marketplace must fundamentally change the very way they think about doing business. In this new global, digital world, the axiom, "change or die," has never been more appropriate.

Global E-business Strategy: Key Components

Communications. Global business is about adapting a company's products and services to meet the varied expectations of markets around the world. A company must also adapt and customize its communications to customers, consumers, suppliers, and others around the world. There exists no common formula to achieve either of these in business today.

Further complicating matters, developing a successful global e-business strategy demands cautious and thorough consideration of linguistic, cultural, economic, and legislative differences in markets around the world. In the past, only the largest companies attempted to create a truly global presence. Companies incapable of competing at this level simply confined themselves to a domestic market, or to a very limited subset of international markets. The Internet and the advent of e-business fundamentally rewrite the rules by wiping out distance, dramatically reducing the barriers of entry to the electronic marketplace, and inciting an atmosphere of hypercompetition on a global level.

Change or die. The Global 500 companies must discard their previously successful strategies or face real danger. Large and small, new and old businesses similarly must struggle with the challenges of how to best conduct business in the new, global digital world.

In the past, businesses adapted their products simply by translating the language on their packaging and their user instructions or by simply changing electrical connectors and voltage to meet local market requirements. Simple language translation or minimal, basic product modifications are not the solutions today.

Business globalization is likewise not simply including existing local cultural and business nuances into a collective global melting pot. A global e-business strategy with its message streaming along the Internet will have to simultaneously provide localized communications to both internal and external users in dozens of different markets while adhering to exacting performance requirements—all this as it processes real-time content changes. Few companies, if any, have mastered this.

The following information will provide companies of all sizes, and most of all, small and midsize companies, a practical road map or template to use as they develop their own global e-business strategy. This information should serve as a checklist of the most critical activities required to successfully deploy a global e-business strategy for any company. The level and depth to which a company will need to go depends largely on the size of the company, the resources it has available, and its vision and aspirations to become truly global.

Global E-business Strategy and Business Plan Development

Any company's globalization strategy can be tremendously enhanced with an effective e-business strategy. To develop a successful e-business globalization strategy, companies of all sizes must first:

- Clearly articulate their overall business and e-business strategies.

- Possess a keen knowledge of their target markets (countries), considering:
  - Geography
  - Demographics
  - Economic conditions
  - Internal country politics
  - The political situation between home and target countries
  - Home and target countries' legal requirements, and
  - Internet readiness.

- Carefully select target markets (countries), groups of markets, etc.

- Plan to establish a company and/or brand identity in target markets.

Also, regardless of the degree of complexity of the company's global e-business strategy, some common traits typically emerge with most, if not all, e-business sites. Specifically, these include:

- Visitors to multiple-language sites remain on the site almost twice as long as they do with English-only language sites.

- Business users are three times more likely to buy when the site is in their own local language.

- Customer service costs decrease when instructions on the site are in the customer's own local language.

Market Selection

A company should prioritize and rank the markets (countries) that may be targeted in its global business strategy. As with all business, developing a global e-business strategy requires that a company know its targeted customer groups very well.

If a company already conducts business in specific markets or if a market is a new high-priority target market, the firm must determine if these markets meet a set of strategic screening criteria. Criteria to be considered are as follows:

For automatic inclusion:

- Markets already accounting for significant company revenue

- Markets where there already is a large e-business presence

- Markets with large physical presences or strategic regional importance (e.g., Brazil in South America, United Kingdom in Europe)

For automatic exclusion:

- Markets not a significant source of current revenue

- Markets not a significant source of future revenue

- Markets whose local laws do not support the necessary intellectual property rights or copyrights

- Markets that are subject to trade embargoes or other internationally imposed sanctions

For markets that do not clearly fall into either of the categories of automatic inclusion or exclusion, a more detailed analysis should be conducted. A rating and ranking mechanism should be developed to prioritize these remaining markets. Any mechanism that is developed should rate and rank markets based on key economic, strategic, or business criteria. Criteria for detailed analysis should include the following:

Economic viability:

- Current market size

- Potential market size

- Current market penetration

- Potential market penetration

- Current market revenue and profit

- Potential market revenue and profit

- Presence or absence of local business and/or brand alliances

- Presence or absence of direct and/or indirect competition

Internet preparedness:

- Current Internet penetration

- Rate of current and forecasted Internet growth

- Projected Internet penetration

- Internet usage (e.g., willingness to conduct business/purchase online)

- Internet infrastructure capabilities

Business capability:

- Size of in-market business presence

- Experience with company/product brand localization

- Existing language translation capabilities

Establish Localization/Regionalization Parameters

A company must establish a set of cultural expectations regarding how a local e-business and Internet presence should perform for each market that a company selects. Based on these local expectations, parameters should then be selected for each market. Sometimes, localization parameters need not apply across all selected markets, but rather they may be applied across a common group of markets in a homogeneous region (e.g., the Middle East). In this case, a regional approach to establishing localization parameters may be more appropriate. Parameters to be considered are:

- Company and/or product/service brand(s)

- Information architecture

- Visual design

- Application functionality

- Content

- Business processes

Establish Globalization Parameters

Once a company has set its localization and regionalization parameters it can establish its globalization parameters. The firm must consider relevant factors from each market. To the extent that any localization feature can be applied on a globalized level, localized or regionalized parameters may then influence and otherwise determine specific globalization parameters. Also, not all localization or regionalization parameters may need to be addressed in the final set of globalization parameters. In some cases, it may be more cost-effective to localize or regionalize some systems without globalizing them. Parameters that should be globalized include: languages, writing systems, currencies, weights and measurements, calendars, time zones, time measurements, and postal and telephone systems.

Languages and phonetic systems. Language is one of the primary differentiators for many cultures. The importance of language clearly makes language-related functions prime targets in implementing global e-business strategy. This is no simple task, however. Languages are extremely diverse, and they change very rapidly.

There are currently 6,700 living languages in the world, but only 435 of these languages are in commercial use. Of all spoken languages, the top 15 in the world together account for 49.5 percent of all the languages spoken by the world's total population. The remaining 51.5 percent of the population speaks more than 6,600 languages among them. At the upper level, there are:

- 100 languages with more than 10 million native speakers

- 20 languages with more than 50 million native speakers

- 8 languages with more than 100 million native speakers

Writing and ideogrammatic systems. Writing systems have a major impact on the way information is presented. Direction of script varies significantly between writing systems. The direction of Latin script is from left to right, top to bottom. The direction of Japanese scripts is generally from top to bottom, right to left, although there can be a mixture of directions on a single page.

Not only does the direction of script vary between systems, but the method used to sort words differs as well. The Latin writing system sorts words and letters using a process based on a fixed sequence called alphabetical order (A to Z). The Japanese hiragana writing system arranges the syllables in the order they appear in a famous Buddhist poem. The Chinese hanzi writing system orders symbols by the number of brush strokes it takes to draw them.

Currencies. Currency is involved in most commerce, and thus is another prime target of global e-business. There are 147 currencies defined by the International Standards Organization. Many markets do not have their own currency; still others accept multiple currencies.

Many potential customers in markets around the world expect to purchase goods using their own currencies. While offering them this service is desirable, it can also expose an organization to considerable risk if not handled correctly.

Currency conversion rates fluctuate on a very short time scale because of trading in global currency markets. This fluctuation makes setting fixed prices in different markets difficult to coordinate. The Internet makes this form of arbitrage even easier.

Weights and measurement systems. Commerce often involves the exchange of fixed quantities of goods or materials that meet certain dimensional specifications. Thus, it is important to consider internationalizing weights and measures. The International System of Units (SI), more commonly referred to as the metric system, is effectively the global standard for measurement. A few markets still cling to old systems: At this time, only three markets—Myanmar, Liberia, and the United States—have not adopted the SI standard as their official system of weights and measures.

The United States is the only industrialized nation that does not mainly use the metric system in its commercial and standards activities, but acceptance is increasing in science, medicine, government, and many sectors of industry in the United States.

Weights and measures present one of the few cases in which establishing a specific parameter course of action is clear. A U.S. company expanding into global markets must embrace the metric system, for the simple reason that no other industrialized market in the world uses the U.S. Customary System. A foreign organization seeking access to American markets must similarly adapt to the U.S. Customary System, or risk alienating U.S. customers or business partners.

For global e-businesses that trade in goods or services based on nonstandard systems, globalization should also be seriously considered.

Calendar systems. Calendars, especially in a global e-business context, are useful in determining holidays, shipment dates, or the date on which a transaction took place. Calendars, like writing systems, come in several varieties. Each calendar determines the number and names of days and months in the year, including when leap years occur.

Three calendar types and at least ten calendars are in daily use around the world. Following are the three calendar types with examples of each:

1. Solar—based on the yearly solar cycle. Examples: Gregorian, Julian, Ethiopic, Coptic, Modern Hindu

2. Lunar—based on the cycle of the moon. Example: Islamic

3. Lunisolar—that attempt to reconcile the cycles of both the sun and moon. Examples: Chinese, Hebrew, Old Hindu

These differences can lead to significant confusion when converting from one calendar to another is required. With today's information technology, the task of reconciling the different calendar systems can be made simpler.

Time zones. Specification of time zones is important for standard time measurement, and could be highly relevant in computer transactions. There are 24 international time zones, and markets set their local time according to the time zone they are in and the time zones adopted by their trading partners and neighbors.

All markets define their own local time in terms of hours ahead or behind Greenwich Mean Time (GMT), up to a maximum of 11 hours ahead or behind. The situation is complicated by the fact that many markets observe daylight saving time, usually hours ahead or behind local time. This is determined at the market level, with different markets beginning and ending daylight saving on different dates (e.g., the U.S. and Canada versus Europe). Individual markets may also vary the start and end dates of daylight saving from year to year, further complicating matters.

Time measurement systems. For certain types of e-business systems, the measurement of accurate time is crucial. This is especially true when systems comprise multiple components distributed geographically. The management of time can become a significant hurdle. Coordinating multiple clocks and managing time changes to and from daylight saving time across multiple time zones requires considerable planning. While these problems may be new to many commercial organizations, they have been recognized and solved by scientific and military institutions.

An example illustrating the need for highly accurate time coordination is in the financial and commodities markets. Most financial and commodity market maker systems that provide auctions also require accurate time synchronization so auctions can close exactly when required and bids can be "time-stamped" with the correct time. Time stamps are also very useful in many cryptographic protocols, where time is intimately connected with the exchange of messages.

Postal systems. The Universal Postal Union (UPU), with headquarters in Bern, Switzerland, is a specialized institution of the United Nations that regulates the postal services of its 189 member countries. This union forms the largest physical distribution network in the world. Some 6.2 million postal employees working in more than 700,000 post offices all over the world handle an annual total of 430 billion letters, printed matter, and parcels in the domestic service and almost 10 billion letters, printed matter, and parcels in the international service.

The UPU is responsible for maintaining a list of national postal addressing systems. The postal addressing systems outline the elements that form the basis for proper postal addressing. These elements ensure the correct wording of addresses and guarantee the quick and efficient handling of letter-post items.

Of the 189 member countries of the UPU, 103 currently have postcode systems in effect (Universal Postal Union 1999). Each country's system is different and is valid only for addresses in that country.

Postcodes can also be used to validate text addresses. Software systems are available that can derive a postcode from a text address and a text address from a postcode. These systems are usually only available with delivery code systems. They require large supporting databases and must be updated frequently to account for new addresses and codes.

Telephone dialing systems. Telephone dialing codes are another means for geographic location; they are quite useful for communication as well. From the standpoint of globalization, it is important to understand the relevant international standards for telecommunications, and also the degree of local variation in the way countries handle telephone numbers.

The Telecommunication Standardization Sector of the International Telecommunications Union (ITU-T) is the Geneva-based United Nations agency responsible for dealing with international telecommunications standards. In the early 1960s, the ITU-T devised a global numbering plan so that the various national telephone systems could be linked; this used country codes of one to three digits in length, assigned according to geographic regions on the earth. For example, Burkina Faso (in Africa) has a country code of 226; France's country code is 33; China's is 86.

Within a specific country, a numbering plan is used to determine how numbers will be allocated. This national numbering plan is usually controlled by a government agency or by the monopoly telephone carrier (if one exists).

In cases where an area code is used, it is usually possible to map this code to a geographical region for which representative geographical coordinates can be determined. For this to be possible, telephone numbers must be recorded in a standard manner. The method recommended by the ITU-T for formatting telephone numbers (ITU 1988) uses the plus sign followed by the country code, then the area code if any, then the local number.

It seems safe to assume that most people are familiar with their domestic number, but not the proper international format. This is important, because there is clearly a wide degree of variation within domestic numbers. Each country breaks digits into groups (although of different lengths); some use parentheses, some use hyphens, some use neither. Any globalized application would have to allow for these variations.

KEY ATTRIBUTES OF A SUCCESSFUL GLOBAL E-BUSINESS STRATEGY

Irrespective of any individual company-specific parameters (globalization, localization/regionalization), company size, industry or markets targeted, a successful global e-business strategy should possess three key attributes: flexibility, adaptability, and controllability.

Flexibility. Localization/regionalization parameters that may apply in one market may not apply in another. Globalization parameters that are critical to support a single major market may undermine the overall strategy and render it cost-ineffective. Typically, most companies find there is no single, correct solution, and that any global e-business strategy will have its trade-offs. In the end, any viable globalization strategy chosen must be flexible across targeted markets.

Adaptability. Everything in the world of business and financial markets changes. International and national politics and laws change, sometimes daily. So, too, does the Internet; and changes seem to be accelerating each year. Any chosen global e-business strategy must be able to adapt to the many changes that have become part of everyday business life, especially on a global level.

Controllability. To ensure the success of any global e-business strategy, a company must exert a high degree of control to implement a stable and manageable global business organization and its resulting structures. This is especially critical when localizing business processes, for local management will likely be charged with implementing and managing market-specific e-business functions.

Cost-Benefit Analysis

Once a company has determined all the criteria with which to establish its global e-business strategies, it must then conduct a cost-benefit analysis to determine the economic viability of the chosen strategies. When analyzing costs, companies must consider both the implementation costs as well as the costs of re-engineering any business processes, ongoing systems maintenance costs, training costs, etc. Once these costs are determined, they can then be weighed against the strategic and economic benefits offered by extending the company's global reach into targeted markets.

Strategy and Business Plan Optimization

If the cost-benefit analysis reveals anything in the global e-business strategy that may be economically viable, a company should consider either adding or removing markets from the mix, modifying some market-specific localization parameters, or adjusting some of its globalization parameters. For example, the cost of globalizing language and writing systems for the Chinese market may be too high, while localization or regionalization is more viable.

Depending on what parameters will be adjusted, added, or removed, it will likely be necessary to review both sets of localized/ regionalized and globalized parameters. Following each series of adjustments, a new cost-benefit analysis should be conducted and the viability of the global e-business strategy reassessed.

Once optimized, the cost-benefit analysis should yield a global e-business strategy that will include the following key elements:

- Prioritized list of markets to be targeted

- Parameters to be localized within the targeted markets

- Requirements mapping of localization and/or regionalization of selected business processes that may be necessary

- Parameters to be globalized within various business systems

- Estimation of costs and benefits of the global e-business strategy

GLOBAL E-BUSINESS STRATEGY IMPLEMENTATION

Once a company has successfully developed and optimized its global e-business strategy, it must develop and execute an implementation plan. Key components of any such implementation plan should include the following:

- Localization/regionalization of business processes as required

- Globalization of business processes as required

- Globalization of appropriate global parameters as required

- Localize globalized parameters within selected markets

- Localize nonglobalized parameters within selected markets

Typically, a phased approach is taken regarding these implementations, with the most strategic markets being implemented first. At the same time, some implementation tasks may be undertaken concurrently with others in selected markets. The ultimate methodology selected by a company will depend on its chosen strategy and the specific challenges presented in each case.

Cultural Adaptability of Global Technology Implementation

Standardized technologies alone won't guarantee successful global e-business operations. The most successful global organizations properly manage multilingual and multicultural implementations of applications and data. Because every successful global e-business implementation must employ components of the technology that require these multilingual and multicultural services and support, companies that specialize in translation, localization, and cultural practices are thriving as part of the global e-business solution. A rudimentary search on the Internet will yield scores of such companies prepared and ready to assist any size company to achieve the desired level of multilingual and multicultural needs that any company may have.

The need to translate and localize foretells that the true challenges in implementing global e-business systems still center on culture, not in the deployment of new technology. In short, everyone can be given the same applications, but ensuring that those applications are used consistently to benefit the company is much more difficult.

By drastically reducing the importance of proximity, the new technologies change people's perceptions of community. The Internet connects people and companies across borders with exponentially growing ease, while separating them from natural and historical associations with nations. Doing business globally filters through many levels of the information technology, local practices, and corporate culture. The more sensitive corporate leadership is toward language and cultural differences, the more an organization is able to improve and add value to its global e-business initiatives.

Buyers and Shippers at CSX are following this approach by encouraging employees to think in terms of information transfer rather than container movement. Staff members must be concerned not only with whether a container made it on board; they must also ensure that purchase orders include all the right information, that goods have been properly tagged for scanning, and that information is in the correct format for electronic transmission. But encouraging new thinking is not enough—performance measures must also change. Buyers and Shippers once measured employee performance and efficiency based on how many phone calls they answered and how many containers they loaded. Today, the company measures effectiveness by assessing how accurate and timely the information is.

That kind of shift in thinking doesn't happen overnight for either employees or managers, regardless of the technology the company employs. Overall company cultures, particularly in local company offices around the world deeply influenced by their individual market cultures, will need to change their mind-sets to make that shift.

Culture—the amalgam of tradition, relationships, and values—shapes business practices and processes in widely varying ways. Cultural differences often make it hard to obtain consensus and collaboration, and not what the "technology of the day" is. The divide between culture, technology, and knowledge can be enormous. To close this divide, successful global organizations of all sizes and cultures realize that a clear understanding of their own company and its home market culture as well as the culture of others is urgently needed.

Cultural Communications in Global E-business Strategy

Cultural differences can make a large impact on the interpretation of visual design. What is considered a cutting-edge design in one culture can appear rude and unprofessional in another. Common interpretations of visual design simply cannot be assumed when working internationally. By their nature, visual messages are often more ambiguous and open to interpretation than is the written word.

Colors. Colors are a part of most people's everyday worlds. We attach a great deal of significance to them, whether we realize it or not. The meanings attached, however, and even the words we use to describe them, vary between cultures. For example, Japanese do not differentiate between green and blue. In the Netherlands, blue connotes quality, and in China, red has negative connotations. Different interpretations of color abound throughout the world.

Image. Images are also interpreted differently across cultures and locations. It is very difficult for a central organization to make appropriate choices about local imagery. Apart from the obvious case where images include text, images themselves often contain cultural assumptions. Images must be made locally appropriate; what appears as an innocuous pictogram of the thumbs-up signal (representing approval) is, in fact, an offensive gesture in some cultures. A car shown driving down the right side of the road would contradict experience in several markets, thus disrupting the intent of a carefully built design.

Colors, images, and text combine to create a graphical interface, and changes to any one of these elements can impact the entire visual design. Text translation can cause significant expansion in the length of text that, in turn, may create a negative impact on a visual design. Substantial modification of text can disrupt the flow of information and qualitatively change the look and feel of an interface. Careful localization of text helps preserve the original intent and spirit of a visual design.

Cultural assumptions affect function in a way similar to information architecture and visual design. As a result, the function of a system may have to be localized to meet cultural requirements. For instance, the concept of the shopping cart on a commercial Web site does not translate for all cultures. The supermarket as a standard for a commercial experience is justified only when most customers experience supermarkets as a regular part of their daily life. Only then will they know what to expect when confronted with the Internet shopping cart.

If an application offers a negative or confusing experience to a user with a different set of cultural expectations, it is no longer useful and thus fails in its intent. Before creating any content (words, images, audio, or video), a company with an Internet presence must first develop a content strategy that articulates the voice and tone of its brand. This strategy ensures that the content is consistent and compelling, and that it properly communicates the message of the brand.

As is the case with information architecture and visual design, the local focus of content must account for subtle and not-so-subtle cultural variations. For example, localizing the audio portions of a Web site requires not only translating the audio into the appropriate language, but accounting for dialect and pronunciation differences. The localization of text requires a similar attention to idiomatic expressions, differences in usage, and culturally specific grammatical conventions.

Language. Language translation is an art, not a science. Literal translation is almost never sufficient. At best, it can produce stilted approximations of the original and, at worst, it can erode a brand's credibility by being unintentionally amusing or even insulting to the target audience and others.

Ensuring text is carefully reviewed by a native speaker is essential even when the text is not ostensibly being translated into another language. In Spain the verb *to take* is perfectly acceptable, while in Mexico it is considered crude. At first glance, a manufacturer may believe that the American version of a product catalog can be reused in all English-speaking markets. This may be the case; the catalog would probably still be understandable. If local language usage is not taken into account, however, it might also cause serious brand erosion. In effect, this means that language and market are inseparable. For example, American, British, Australian, Canadian, and South African English should be treated as separate languages. Each market has its own language variation that must be handled individually.

Another factor to consider when localizing text is that translation can have a significant, even damaging, effect on visual design and information architecture. When text is translated, the amount of space required to hold that contiguous block of text can change dramatically. On the average, English increases by 30 percent when it is translated to other European languages, and can increase by 400 percent in extreme cases.

SUMMARY

Leaders of small and midsize companies planning to compete on a global scale are already searching for ways to more quickly leverage new information technologies and the Internet to create their global e-business strategies. But even with these advancements, and all the imperatives to make IT the core component of the corporation's global strategy, many of these leaders may still view the world of global IT and e-business with some degree of skepticism and even fear. Many of these leaders believe they have been burned by huge investments in IT infrastructure projects whose promise far outweighed the results. As a result, they may become conservative and reluctant to invest any more, despite knowing intuitively that it is IT and the Internet that will enable their companies to become global. Many may be uneasy with continuing high IT investments. Moreover, some of these leaders may simply be wary because they are either uninformed or unconvinced of the true potential of IT and the Internet as the key driver of their company's globalization strategy.

For many, global e-business strategies have also become much more complex, making such initiatives appear to be even more risky than they really are. In the 1990s, IT strategies focused on replacing outdated information systems and reducing cycle times as well as on related transaction costs. Today, strategies have been expanded to implement global communications systems in multiple languages that accommodate the needs of disparate customers, suppliers, and strategic partners on a worldwide basis. Couple this with the addition of the cultural and linguistics complexities inherent in such an undertaking and it is easy to understand the reluctance of company executives to move forward aggressively with their global e-business strategies.

Ironically, it is now, in this precise time in global manifest destiny's decelerated proactivity phase, that companies should be moving forward aggressively with their global e-business strategies. It is now that real progress in globalizing business can be made.

CHAPTER 7

GLOBAL PROCUREMENT

Global procurement is an instrumental component to the strategic mix for companies looking to grow their business worldwide. It can also offer tremendous opportunities to companies along the way. Low costs of foreign products and services can enable smaller firms to become more competitive, increase sales, and increase profits. Buying in global markets that are abundant in natural resources can alleviate raw materials shortages. The availability of a specific technology and/or a cheap, but trainable and increasingly reliable, labor force abroad could overcome some manufacturing and financial problems. Small and midsize companies, specifically, need to lower raw material and supply costs to successfully compete with their larger competitors with their economies of scale and volume purchase discounts that smaller companies don't have.

When a company decides to expand its presence abroad, its global marketing objectives often can be better served through an effective global procurement strategy, i.e., access to more and lower prices from a more diverse and geographically dispersed group of suppliers. Benefits of a global procurement strategy are further evident in the trends in foreign trade. According to the trends, scarce resources, technological innovations, and competition throughout the world should cut down artificial barriers to foreign trade in the future and political boundaries for economic purposes should become relatively less visible. Global procurement, consequently, will become an integral part of the company's overall global corporate strategy, regardless of the size of the company. In short, it is virtually impossible to seriously compete in today's business, domestically or globally, by confining buying to solely domestic sources.

During the late 1990s and into mid-2001 at the time of this writing, the strength of the U.S. dollar made purchasing foreign-made goods that much cheaper for U.S. companies, which helped drive America's price competitiveness even higher. At the same time, the strong U.S. dollar also made it much more difficult for these same U.S. companies to compete at home and abroad. In any case, global procurement, if carried out properly, provides a company with more competitive tools which it can utilize as different situations arise. Without such wide access to suppliers around the globe, a company could easily find itself at a competitive disadvantage both home and abroad, especially during times when it experiences a strong domestic currency.

Periods of exceptionally strong and weak currency swings impact all companies, as well as all customers and consumers. These times ultimately affect the national economy and the entire world economy. Despite concern over the U.S. balance of trade deficits, national pride, and unemployment problems, companies of all sizes will have to look to global markets to be successful, and will need sophisticated purchasing professionals to deal with the new challenges of global procurement and capitalize on its tremendous and varied benefits.

In this chapter we will explore the need for all companies to transform their domestic-focused purchasing organizations into true global procurement experts. This is the challenge, for historically the role of purchasing in business has played a less-than-strategic role for most companies.

PURCHASING TAKES ON
A NEW ROLE: PROCUREMENT

Previously, purchasing as a discipline never attracted the best and the brightest from the ranks of M.B.A. graduates from top-rated business schools, or from any business schools for that matter. In fact, for years purchasing was viewed as a dead-end career path chosen by many who just couldn't succeed in the faster-paced areas of marketing, sales, and finance. Even the tradition-bound engineering and manufacturing groups seemed cutting edge to those in the purchasing department—the department to whom these more strategic groups pass turnkey product specs so purchasing could haggle over pricing and other terms with suppliers already chosen by another one of the more strategic groups in the company. Not until the mid-1990s did companies even begin to think of purchasing departments as contributors to a company's overall business success.

Soon senior executives began to truly understand concepts such as supply chain and total cost of acquisition, and how buyers needed to play more active roles in their relationships with suppliers to reduce costs throughout the entire supply chain. Before long, purchasing professionals were responsible for delivering millions of dollars and more each year to the company's overall profitability through forced reductions in purchasing prices exacted from suppliers. And as the world's economy began to conduct business with more and more companies of all sizes, the stakes became even greater for purchasing professionals. Now they were forced to look beyond their domestic borders and learn to play an entirely new game, the game of global procurement. With the opening of the world's economy now coinciding with the simultaneous ramp-up of the Internet, the stakes of global procurement were instantly raised. Global procurement emerged as a critical cog in the company's overriding business strategy to expand its entire range of operations to the far reaches of the world and to attain the status of a true global company.

As we will discuss in this chapter, the role of the global procurement professional requires an in-depth understanding of everything from global finance to global logistics, global product category management to global manufacturing and operations, global supply chain integration, global e-business, and, finally, global supplier relationship management. Obviously, times have dramatically changed, for today, any top-flight M.B.A. from any one of the best business schools would be severely challenged with this intellectual workload and responsibility.

WHAT IS GLOBAL PROCUREMENT?

In today's global business economy, many purchasing professionals are diving headlong into global procurement—whether they are ready for it may be another matter. While the basic task is the same whether a company is buying domestically or globally, the global transaction is significantly more complex. At a time when the complexities of conducting global business are growing exponentially, creating a potential encumbrance on a company's cost structures, global procurement is now capable of bringing real value to the global company by leveraging purchases and creating cost efficiencies.

Global trends such as outsourcing and extending the business enterprise across the world are making the integration of interbusiness processes a high priority for many organizations. While many companies have undergone strategic sourcing transformations, they have stopped after rationalizing the supply base and negotiating new prices or have not even attempted to take these new processes offshore to the extent that they should.

True collaboration requires seamless communication and transaction processes on a global basis with suppliers wherever they are conducting business—collaboration that eliminates costs from the entire global procurement process rather than moving them down the supply chain.

Current procurement practices are often ineffective and inefficient either domestically or globally. Often, paper-based procurement processes are still the norm in many organizations. As a result of incomplete information, errors, incorrect routing, and delays, these processes are time-consuming and costly. It is also difficult to get up-to-date pricing and availability information and is virtually impossible to track orders. Purchase orders can take weeks to move from requisition to approval to invoices that need even longer processing time.

New developments in e-procurement mean streamlining and automating each stage of the process wherever it is in the world, from searching for a product or service to ordering, approval, tracking, and payment in any currency and in virtually any bank in the world. Thus, significant improvements have been realized from the introduction of e-procurement on the global scale. Transaction processing costs and times are reduced upstream as well as downstream, freeing up procurement professionals to perform more value-adding tasks, and reducing maverick and uncoordinated purchasing, thus keeping purchase prices low.

These maverick purchases are made because of the frustration caused by inefficient and/or ineffective purchasing processes. Unless people are able to quickly locate, order, and receive what they need, goods and services will be ordered from unapproved suppliers. This is compounded, sometimes exponentially on the global scale, as enforcing company-wide global compliance becomes extremely challenging. These purchases lower volume leverage with approved suppliers and result in higher prices. According to General Electric Information Services (GEIS) and the Gartner Group, about 30 percent of maintenance, repairs, and operations (MRO) procurement takes place outside negotiated supplier contracts, increasing costs by as much as 20 percent and 50 percent.

Strategic sourcing is the first, but not final, step in achieving collaboration. It is a philosophy and framework that extends beyond the traditional purchasing approach by building and leveraging the extended enterprise. The new strategic relationships and the extended enterprise rely heavily on tight integration and improved processes to realize the true benefits, and the source selection components of strategic sourcing projects must be supplemented with process and technology improvements to allow connectivity and collaboration with any supplier in the global integrated supply chain.

Global procurement, obviously, is a complex and interrelated set of disciplines that require a high degree of careful coordination and sophisticated management. It is a function within the new global company that has come of age and is finally gaining the respect and attention of executive management among other critical functional areas within the global company—respect and attention that is needed to assist executive management in fulfilling their company's rich global destiny.

DEVELOPING A GLOBAL PROCUREMENT STRATEGY

The development of any global procurement strategy centers on three key components regardless of the size of the company or the industry in which it operates:

1. Global supply chain integration

2. Global e-procurement

3. Global strategic supplier alliances

For the balance of this chapter, we will examine each one of these key components to better understand what organizations must do with respect to global procurement if they seek to establish themselves as true global companies.

Global Supply Chain Integration

There are as many definitions of supply chain management as there are supply chain managers, but a basic definition involves three main components: obtaining information to run the global business, delivering products to customers around the world, and getting cash to generate profits from anywhere in the world. The cash can be in the form of rubles, deutsche marks, Japanese yen, or U.S. dollars. In a global economy, however, the task is not complete until the currency is in the correct form. Under the old organizational structure, production and inventory managers left that responsibility to finance managers. Today, global procurement and its supply chain managers look at the business of the company in the aggregate, and cross-disciplinary decision making is replacing functional silos in all their markets globally.

Integrated supply chain management requires using a holistic approach when making business decisions. As stated previously, global procurement executives need to be very skilled in international finance for they must develop strategies so their organizations can build strong links with their trading partners by applying sound international financial management concepts. If the goal is to create a competitive advantage from the network of trading partners, decisions must be made at the chain level, not strictly at the individual company level.

All companies in the integrated global supply chain must pay special attention to currency exchange, capital financing, and synergy. By addressing the process of currency exchange and the types of risk involved for each link in the supply chain, the total chain costs can be reduced. Opportunities can be found to leverage the global supply chain to create capital financing for all the links in the global supply chain. The objective of maximizing shareholders' current and future wealth has not changed; companies, however, should look internally and externally at all the links in the chain to find the competitive advantage that supports these objectives.

Assembling the global supply chain. A global supply chain consists of trading partners from the supplier's supplier to the customer's customer. The chain becomes global when international boundaries are crossed, and the interaction becomes more dynamic. Logistics, taxes, quotas, language barriers, culture barriers, government restrictions, and currency issues all add to the complexity of global trade.

Organizations are driven into global trade by the pressure for cost reduction from the customer and by the ability to access new markets. In every industry, to gain a competitive advantage, companies attempt to develop a global network that will outperform rival networks.

An example from the wireless communications industry illustrates the interrelated and integrated financial links that evolve from a global supply chain. A European mobile phone manufacturer ordered electronic components and assemblies from an Asian subcomponent manufacturer based in Hong Kong. Decisions regarding exact quantities and part numbers were not initially determined; at the same time, anticipated demand was communicated up and down the supply chain by the European manufacturer to its Hong Kong supplier. Based on the best configuration to meet the customer's needs, the Hong Kong–based company then routed the work through a global network of its own suppliers. The electronic components and assemblies manufacturer purchased some raw material in Korea, and then others in Taiwan. Some parts were transferred to Thailand for subassembly, and the electronic subassemblies were in the European mobile phone manufacturer's final assembly location within five weeks from the start of production.

This supply chain required five currency exchanges. Logistics aside, the transaction is financially complex. The correct quantity of Korean won, Japanese yen, Taiwan yuan, and Thai baht had to be in the right place at the right time. Euros had to be converted to Hong Kong dollars to complete the transaction.

Although electronic commerce improves the velocity of these transactions, financial planning is necessary to cover this transaction and the many similar transactions that surround it. Inventory managers, as managers of critical corporate resources, strive to provide the correct amount of material at the correct place at the correct time at the least cost. Financial managers face a similar challenge with another corporate resource—cash. And all of this must be coordinated and managed by the global procurement professional.

Global E-procurement

For many companies, global e-procurement can transform worldwide procurement by streamlining and automating each stage of the process, from searching for a product or service to ordering, approval, tracking, and payment. Components such as online catalogs, intelligent purchasing agents, intranet work flow, extranet team rooms, and online auctions are making traditional communication channels, such as fax and electronic data interchange (EDI) redundant. But what really is global e-procurement all about?

Global e-procurement is simply companies buying their supplies online from suppliers in multiple markets. It centers on turning paper-based processes into Internet transactions and moving from the one-to-one technology of the old EDI systems to Internet-based networks. While much of the early hype concerned open e-marketplaces, i.e., virtual Web sites where anyone could come to buy or sell a particular range of goods, the trend now is toward closed communities centered on a particular global customer or supplier.

Significant improvements have been realized from the introduction of e-procurement, especially when applied at the global level with its inherent complexities of great distances and diverse languages, cultures, currencies, local trade regulations, etc. Transaction processing costs and times are reduced, freeing up global procurement professionals to perform more value-added tasks, and streamlining and automation reduce maverick—unnecessary or spontaneous—purchasing, keeping purchase prices low.

With most global companies spending at least one-third of their overall budget to purchase goods and services, savings generated from a comprehensive global e-procurement approach on total company purchases approximate between 2 percent and 12 percent, representing a significant value to the business.

Some companies are now using global e-procurement to make as much as 90 percent of all company purchases electronically and to gather market intelligence, set price points, and communicate and collaborate with suppliers in a shared electronic workspace. Many companies are saving critical dollars by being able to determine at all times the supply and demand status of purchased goods, thus allowing them to leverage worldwide volumes and negotiate more effectively. As a result, companies increasingly rely on their strategic suppliers around the globe to provide value-added contributions rather than just products to their overall value proposition.

Purchasing Magazine has estimated that global purchasing managers spend more than 35 percent of their time on routine paperwork. The inherent automation and efficiency of global e-procurement frees up this time so these managers can tackle more important, value-adding issues such as strategic sourcing and supplier management. For many companies, this results in impressive cost savings and quality improvements that drop to the bottom line.

E-procurement provides quicker product development times, faster access to available goods and services, easier ordering, shipment tracking, management control, and faster delivery—and on a global basis, which is especially important. It reduces the total costs by integrating and automating each step of the process around the world. It also reduces inventory costs by improving the tracking of products and reduces the need for safety stocks by building confidence anywhere in the world.

Global e-procurement also improves the ability to search and find the best source of a given product, and ensures that only products from approved suppliers are purchased. Global e-procurement benefits sellers by increasing their product visibility to prospective buyers and presenting their products and services in a more compelling way.

One of the main drivers to e-procurement is the opportunity it affords companies to restructure relationships with suppliers from all around the globe. But the cost-slashing aspect can rebound and hurt a company because of the potential reduced choice of suppliers, for the customer is now committed to dealing only with the suppliers who go through its e-procurement network. In any case, if the procurement department has been doing its job properly, the per-unit purchase costs should be down.

Cost-cutting aims are achieved through supply chain restructuring and integration rather than e-procurement alone. But when e-procurement is joined with a comprehensive strategic global procurement initiative to drive costs down, it facilitates consolidation of total purchasing expenditure, renegotiation with suppliers, and then discussion about integrating the selected supplier into the global e-procurement process. In other words, rather than global e-procurement being the driver of the process, it is the enabler.

As with any open and integrated system with many freely acting participants, a number of risk factors must be considered when developing any global e-procurement strategy. By definition, any open marketplace makes it difficult to quantify risk and identify contractual responsibilities. As e-procurement technology continues to evolve, it increasingly creates different buying and selling scenarios. When a company establishes its markets, it usually does so around a number of different structures. Some intermediary—a company's agent, wholesaler, or a facilitator not involved in the contractual process at all—may create a problem. Thus, even though contractual relationships must be closely analyzed, the "people" side of the enterprise must not be ignored. Even with all the sophisticated technology, people still make decisions and commitments to each other on behalf of their companies, and the question always remains whether those agreements and commitments will be honored.

For this reason, companies of all sizes embarking on the global e-procurement path must establish close working relationships with e-procurement suppliers in new strategic supplier alliances, and at the same time, accept more superficial relationships with suppliers out there in a marketplace trading with the company on a one-time-only basis.

Many options must be considered, and a company's global e-procurement solution should be selected to match its own business processes and the requirements of its customers or suppliers. In the next section in this chapter, we will address this exact point, and, in particular, the development and ongoing management of the critical strategic supplier alliance with the company's selected global suppliers.

Global Strategic Supplier Alliances

As the nature of the global competitive environment changes, the interest in various types of alliances has grown. Many successful firms are turning away from adversarial relationships with trading partners and are relying increasingly on parties outside the firm. Furthermore, as companies look more frequently to the purchasing function to help them meet their cost and quality goals, the possibility of forming alliances with suppliers has become an area of great interest to many firms.

A strategic supplier alliance differs from traditional supplier or vendor relationships because it involves an inherent trust, as well as a mutual commitment and sharing. Firms are interested in forming such alliances rather than adversarial relationships because these alliances offer more advantages. A strategic supplier alliance is a logical development if the supplier base has been reduced, if quality and dependability are critical, or if the quality of suppliers varies. An alliance may also be important if the supplier's system is tightly coupled with the company's manufacturing system.

Attributes of a true strategic supplier alliance include:

- Tight operating links, such as product development coordination, integration of systems and processes

- Collaboration on value-added projects and programs to reduce and avoid common operating costs

- Long-term contracts based on quality and service, not just price

- Mutual vested interest in each other's future

- Executive commitment and support; high frequency of contact at executive and middle levels of management

- Reciprocal relationships sharing strengths, information, and mutual advantages

Some of the potential advantages of forming global procurement alliances over traditional international purchasing relationships include:

1. Reduced supplier base is easier to manage.

2. Increased mutual dependence lowers the risk of losing supply source and creates greater stability through increased supplier loyalty.

3. Reduces time looking for new suppliers/gathering competitive bids.

4. Allows for joint planning and information sharing based on mutual trust and benefit.

5. Loyalty may increase supplier retention and customer service in areas such as:

   - Lead-time reliability
   - Priority in times of scarcity
   - Increased attention when problems arise.

6. Greater cooperation from suppliers supports the company's strategy.

7. Alliance partners may be more willing to share/give access to technology.

8. Alliance partners may be more willing and capable of participating in product design based on knowledge and commitment to the other partner.

9. Supplier knowledge/involvement in design may improve quality and reduce time to market for new products/design changes.

10. Global procurement alliance partners may share business risks through:

    - Joint investment
    - Joint research and development
    - Sharing of financial risks associated with market shifts.

Developing Alliances with Strategic Global Suppliers

Establishing a need for a strategic supplier alliance is a critical first step. This need is generally identified by executive management—based on competitive strategy and an environmental assessment—and incorporated into the firm's strategic plan. Or the need may come from procurement or another functional area and filter up through the organization to executive management.

After the need is determined, five steps are involved in the development process. These include: identifying potential partners, evaluating suppliers, selecting the supplier, establishing a relationship with suppliers, and monitoring the relationship.

Step 1: Identify potential global strategic supplier alliance partners. Identifying potential partners for global strategic supplier alliances involves determining the selection criteria and identifying a list of potential alliance partners. While these criteria include traditional supplier selection criteria, such as cost, quality, availability, and so on, they go substantially beyond the factors considered in the traditional bidding process.

Criteria regarding the long-term positioning of the alliance partner and management and cultural compatibility, while highly judgmental, are important in establishing the long-term viability of the relationship.

With the criteria for selection clearly established, a list of potential supplier alliance partners should be developed based on those capable of meeting the company's supply needs. This list may include suppliers with whom the company has had previous experience, as well as suppliers with whom it has not dealt directly. This list of potential suppliers may come from purchasing, engineering, quality assurance, and any other functions with knowledge about specific suppliers.

Obviously, unsuitable candidates should be eliminated early, because exploring each potential supplier is a time-consuming process. Unsuitable candidates usually include those with whom the company has had unsatisfactory experience in the past. If a company does not want to commit to substantial capital investment, companies with inadequate capacity and technology may also be ruled out. This phase may progress rapidly if the company is extensively experienced in the area and knows potential suppliers. Without this experience and knowledge, this phase can be a slow, iterative process.

Step 2: Evaluate potential global strategic suppliers. After selection criteria and a reasonable list of potential global strategic suppliers has been developed, the potential alliance partners must be evaluated. The number of potential strategic suppliers chosen will depend on the importance of the item under consideration, the number of suppliers capable of supplying the item, the time available for screening suppliers, the amount of time the suppliers may need to develop the item, and so on.

After this screening process, each potential strategic supplier should be approached to assess its interest in the business. Corporate procurement generally performs the initial contact. At the same time, progressive suppliers may also initiate the first contact. Only those suppliers expressing sincere interest in establishing a long-term commitment in an alliancing partnership should be pursued.

Once a potential strategic supplier has determined its capabilities and cost structure for supplying the identified products or services, the customer must decide whether further evaluation of the supplier is warranted. The ultimate choice will be based on the perceived availability, quality, and overall fit of this supplier versus other suppliers. Further consideration of a global strategic supplier involves making a detailed financial and operating analysis, visiting plant locations, and developing a thorough understanding of the supplier's global operations.

Step 3: Select the global strategic supplier. When selecting a global strategic supplier, care must be taken not to focus too much on any one particularly attractive attribute. For example, while its offering of low cost or outstanding quality may be very enticing, the company may have an unstable labor or management base, or it may be financially unstable. Thus, a systematic, integrated approach to evaluating each global supplier is needed. Executive management should generally have input, or at least an awareness of the final suppliers under consideration—again, to maintain its support and commitment to the proposed supplier alliance.

Each global strategic supplier should be evaluated using the same criteria so that the evaluations are directly comparable. The strategic supplier chosen for a supplier alliance should be the one that best meets the company's overall needs. Furthermore, an alliance partner should meet, or appear to be able to meet, all the company's needs at some minimally acceptable level, albeit a high level because of the nature of the deep commitments that will be made. If no acceptable alliance partners are available at this point, the company may wish to return to the previous phase and then evaluate additional potential alliance partners. Alternatively, the company may choose not to seek a strategic supplier alliance relationship, but instead may use competitive bidding, produce the items in-house, or use some other means of procuring the needed product(s).

Step 4: Establish the relationship with strategic global suppliers. This phase of a strategic supplier alliance implementation is an art as much as it is a science. The goal is to establish the foundation on which to build a strong, ongoing relationship based on mutual trust, sharing, and commitment. A partnership will work only if it is beneficial to both parties. Thus, the actual interactions with the global supply partner are critical in determining the future of the relationship. In fact, it all begins with a shared vision between customer and strategic supplier that includes the following attributes:

- Real, solid, and tangible—bottom-line oriented

- Jointly developed through strong collaboration and trust

- Achieved only if customer and supplier think and act as one

- Has the potential to dramatically transform the business of both

- Able to achieve success not possible if either acts alone:
  - Technology breakthroughs
  - New market creation
  - Capture of existing markets not before attainable

- Redefines the relationship between customer and supplier

To prevent misunderstanding, especially when dealing with firms that may have different languages and customs, early clarification of expectations is critical. Establishing expectations in writing may be desirable, not to be used as a pressure tactic, but to clarify needs and expectations. The written document could include items such as key contacts at each company in the alliance, any technology to be shared or mutually developed, handling of proprietary information, frequency of forecast updates, basis for price changes, etc. The more commonality that is in the initial understanding, the less opportunity for problems to develop later. This is true when communicating within the global customer's own organization regarding the alliance relationship, as well as when dealing directly with the global alliance partner.

While a great deal of intercompany interactions may occur among many functional areas, central coordination is required to keep the relationship operating smoothly and consistently. Establishing a critical relationship such as a strategic supplier alliance requires a high initial attention level. Even if a large geographical distance exists, it should not prevent frequent interaction. Interaction is important to establishing a good rapport with the alliance partner early in the relationship. Meetings between the executive management of both companies are desirable to confirm and to demonstrate the high level of mutual commitment of the companies to the success of the alliancing relationship. Key personnel should visit a strategic supplier early in the relationship to better understand the global supplier's facilities and capabilities, and to establish face-to-face contact between parties that will have frequent interaction.

Regardless of potentially long distances and time differences, it is important to interact regularly in the early stages of the relationship to establish the lines of communication. Furthermore, if problems occur in the alliancing relationship, the issues should be addressed quickly to prevent further misunderstanding and to keep the relationship on track.

Step 5. Monitor the relationship with strategic global suppliers. A supplier evaluation should be performed on an ongoing basis. In some companies, alliance partners that meet or exceed all the company's performance expectations receive special recognition. They may become a "certified," "approved," or "preferred" supplier, or they may receive an award. The highest level achieved by any supplier is "strategic supplier" in the customer's strategic supplier alliance, as shown in the strategic supplier alliance evolution (see Figure 7.1). In the strategic supplier alliance, the supplier evolves from a purveyor of products and services, i.e., a *vendor,* and then becomes a *preferred supplier,* i.e., on the shortlist with one or two other suppliers; and finally it is elevated to the level of *strategic supplier,* or the exclusive supplier, or one of two very valued suppliers of a customer's purchases in a specific product or service category.

Based on the outcome of the team's evaluation of supplier performance, several alternative courses of action may be pursued:

- Continue to monitor the supplier relationship, while maintaining it at its current level. The customer may want to

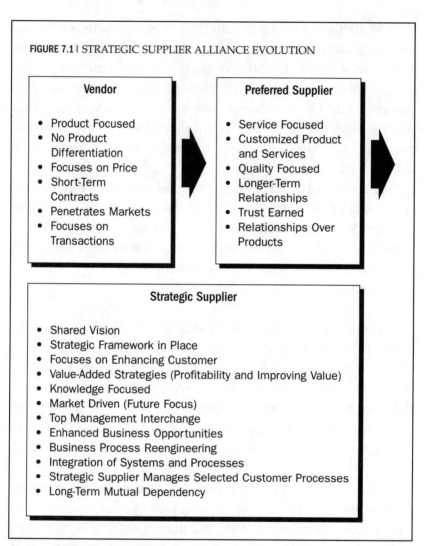

FIGURE 7.1 | STRATEGIC SUPPLIER ALLIANCE EVOLUTION

Vendor

- Product Focused
- No Product Differentiation
- Focuses on Price
- Short-Term Contracts
- Penetrates Markets
- Focuses on Transactions

Preferred Supplier

- Service Focused
- Customized Product and Services
- Quality Focused
- Longer-Term Relationships
- Trust Earned
- Relationships Over Products

Strategic Supplier

- Shared Vision
- Strategic Framework in Place
- Focuses on Enhancing Customer
- Value-Added Strategies (Profitability and Improving Value)
- Knowledge Focused
- Market Driven (Future Focus)
- Top Management Interchange
- Enhanced Business Opportunities
- Business Process Reengineering
- Integration of Systems and Processes
- Strategic Supplier Manages Selected Customer Processes
- Long-Term Mutual Dependency

Source: © Andrew-Ward International, Inc.

pursue this course of action if the relationship has been shaky but is improving. The customer may also choose to maintain the alliancing relationship if the relationship is proceeding well, but the global customer has no need for additional items from the supplier at this time.

- Further build or expand the alliancing relationship. The global customer may want to further develop the alliancing relationship with the global supplier if the supplier has been performing well, and there are other areas in which the global customer believes the supplier could perform well based on the supplier's technology and capability. Alternatively, the global customer may choose to expand the supplier relationship if other, nonalliance partnership suppliers are currently getting part of the business in this area, and the global customer now feels comfortable shifting more of its business to the strategic supplier alliance partner.

- Dissolve or reduce the scope of the relationship with this strategic supplier, as it may now be questionable whether the relationship is any longer strategic in nature. The global customer may decide to either reduce its volume with this supplier or eliminate business with this supplier completely if the supplier is not performing well or many problems exist in the relationship. The relationship should be dissolved only if the parties have made a sincere effort to reconcile any problems they have. Additionally, a strategic supplier alliance may be dissolved or reduced in scope, even if it is functioning well, because the basic business need no longer exists. For example, the supplier may discontinue making a product, or the technology may become obsolete. If the alliance partners have been communicating well over time, this type of dissolution or reduction should come as no surprise to either party.

Dissolving a strategic supplier alliance because of unsatisfactory performance is the least desirable alternative, but it may be necessary. If the customer did its homework properly, problems of nonperformance or culture clash should be relatively rare. Company goals and key players do change, however, so major problems cannot be prevented entirely. The global customer must keep in mind that a customer that abandons supplier alliance partners without a sincere effort to resolve problems may soon develop a reputation, and perhaps other potential supplier alliance partners may be less willing and more suspicious of forming alliances with the customer.

Alliances, or close sharing relationships between a buying and a supplying company, are not a new concept. These relationships have existed for years, and are considered commonplace in other cultures such as in Europe and Japan. Strategic supplier alliances are not fads in these markets, but rather are ways to gain a competitive edge and benefit from the mutual dependency of trading partners. These close working relationships have even been viewed as factors that have increased the competitiveness of these markets in relation to the United States.

Most businesspeople experienced in doing business internationally would generally agree that businesses based in countries in the developed and developing world tend to focus more on building longer-term and deeper relationships in business than do many businesses based in the United States. Simply stated, many U.S.-based companies tend to be more transactional in their business relationships than their European or Asian cultural counterparts.

This is not to say that U.S.-based companies are necessarily doing anything substantially wrong. After all, the United States is the largest economy on the planet, and its companies represent a majority of the leading companies in the world. Rather, there may be potentially new competitive advantages for some U.S.-based companies by the development of more and deeper strategic supplier alliances than what some of these companies are doing today. This is especially true of those companies that tend to have a more transactional business culture than many of their European or Asian competitors.

Furthermore, as the world economy continues to become more interactive globally, and U.S.-based companies increasingly compete head-to-head with foreign companies that use strategic supplier alliances, U.S. companies will need to form alliances to enjoy the same competitive advantages.

As competitors seek alliances with global suppliers, companies will risk losing attractive suppliers to the competition unless they form strategic supplier alliances with those suppliers. Thus, a wait-and-see attitude could result in the erosion of a customer's supply base. Supplier alliance partnerships, however, need not be formed for every purchased ingredient or component. The decision to form such a strategic supplier alliance is exceptional, and relatively few customers and suppliers achieve such a level in their overall buyer-seller relationships. If one alliance partner offers no advantage over another, and enough good suppliers are available that the global customer does not gain by forming an alliance, there may well be no reason to form an alliance. Such an assessment should be made analytically, however, rather than by ignoring the potential of strategic supplier partnering alliances.

Rather than create the risk of a one-sided dependence where the global customer is at the mercy of the supplier, it may make sense to form global strategic supplier alliances. These special supplier alliances recognize and create a mutual dependence that helps develop a more balanced relationship.

SUMMARY

Today's global business economy has many purchasing professionals diving headlong into global procurement—whether they are ready for it may be another matter. While the basic task is the same whether a company is buying domestically or globally, the global transaction is significantly more complex. At a time when the complexities of conducting global business are growing exponentially and creating excessive weight on a company's cost structures, global procurement is now capable of bringing real value to the global company by leveraging purchases and creating cost efficiencies. Global procurement is a complex and interrelated set of disciplines that require a high degree of careful coordination and sophisticated management. It is a function with the new global company that has come of age and is finally gaining the respect and attention of executive management among other critical functional areas within the global company—respect and attention that is needed to assist executive management in fulfilling their company's global destiny.

CHAPTER 8

GLOBAL OPERATIONS

The rapid integration of the world's commercial environment is dramatically changing the face of global business operations. Companies now must take into account not only traditional operational issues such as capacity, facilities, and technology, but also new issues that will affect overall global business strategies.

Global operations, in contrast to the blue-collar image of just a decade ago, have become a fundamental issue for a company's global competitiveness. Global operations now play a major role in global business process implementation and strategic capability development.

In the face of growing global competition, traditional patterns of domestic manufacture and export are increasingly being replaced by global networks of operational capacity. Even if companies are not presently organized globally, they are increasingly likely to need to be able to understand and operate within the global networks established by their global customers.

WHAT IS GLOBAL OPERATIONS MANAGEMENT?

The effective management of global operations involves the ability to move products and services between multicontinental locations swiftly and reliably to ensure the successful servicing of emerging global customer networks.

Traditionally, the strategic assessment of moving products and services has concentrated on the financial aspect alone. This analysis is frequently one-dimensional and is based only on a limited range of variables, such as the cost of a single factor like ocean or air freight. On the other hand, considerably less emphasis is placed on the potential for providing real customer value, while absorbing some of the higher costs.

DEVELOPING A GLOBAL OPERATIONS STRATEGY

When embarking on a global operations strategy, companies must first thoroughly understand the critical activities involved in the process. These activities include:

- Scale of global operations

- Location of global operations

- Global manufacturing configurations

- Logistical options in global operations

Scale of Global Operations

The scale of a company's global operations depends on several factors, both internal and external. Each of these must be analyzed within the context of the company's overall global strategy:

- Transportation costs

- Duties on components versus those on finished goods

- Need for proximity to the market

- Foreign-exchange risk

- Economies of scale in the production process

- Technological requirements

Each one of these directly impacts the location of global operations.

Location of Global Operations

To remain competitive in the global business environment, many firms find it necessary to locate their manufacturing facilities in several countries. The selection of the most appropriate location in which to manufacture products is therefore a major decision that influences the firm's competitive advantage.

The range of factors and issues involved in the process makes the manufacturing location decision one of the most difficult tasks for managers. Decision areas include where to locate a new plant, which plant to close, and where to relocate an existing plant.

Global Manufacturing Configurations

Global manufacturing configurations can be technology-driven, marketing-intensive, or low-cost driven.

In more and more rapidly expanding markets, *technology-driven* products are becoming commoditized frighteningly fast. Companies that once could expect a year or more of market leadership from their investments in new products and technologies now may see that time shrink to a few months or to a few weeks. It's critical that these companies with very high technology investments develop the processes to enable them to enjoy the cash-flow return from their new products for a reasonable time while their competitors try to catch up.

The resulting demands for quicker product launches hugely depend for their success on developing and utilizing quality systems disciplines and technology, which create shorter quality-time cycles but nonetheless provide complete quality discipline to assure fully successful product-launch customer performance. Recognizing and meeting this demand are now becoming basic keys to accomplishing the significant time-cycle reductions in product design and development, production, supplier establishment and integration, and distribution and service required by high-technology industries throughout the world.

If the product or service is *marketing-intensive,* the key is to develop a global operations program that includes a high-quality product and prompt delivery. Traditionally, companies relied on the developed infrastructures of industrialized nations to ensure quality. Because of growth and progress in emerging economies, however, infrastructures have been created that allow manufacturing processes to take place with a higher degree of quality assurance. In many ways, China and Korea have replaced Japan as manufacturing bases for many of the world's most respected quality brands.

If the product or service is *low-cost,* the manufacturing strategy is to use large-scale manufacturing to reduce unit costs or to rely on cheap labor.

Manufacturing outside the borders of a particular country often occurs in low-cost locations and is followed by importation into the targeted markets. Market conditions also can affect offshore production-sharing strategies. For example, a *maquiladora* is an operation in Mexico to which components are shipped from the United States duty-free for assembly and the goods are then reexported to the United States.

Quality is certainly a relevant issue when deciding on which global manufacturing considerations to choose. More and more consumers are making quality their primary purchasing standard, as compared with ten years ago when price and other factors were the primary considerations. But the even more fundamental and rapidly developing change is that these buyers are no longer expressing their concept of quality as primarily functions, dimensions, or characteristics of a product or attributes of a service, but they are instead integrating quality with value. They are approaching quality as a fundamental buying discipline measured by their total value perception of the product or service they are considering purchasing as well as of the organization, delivery, and maintenance network that provides and supports it. Quality has many dimensions, such as zero defects, which was perfected first by Japanese manufacturers who refused to tolerate defects of any kind.

Exploring joint ventures. In today's global market the opportunity for joint venture arrangements has increased considerably. A joint venture should be considered a contractual marriage with a specific purpose or purposes. The joint venture agreement is important, but there may also be security, subscribing, management, cash-flow, or other specific agreements. For example, two entities from two different countries may have a target investment in a third country. Both investors will look for a neutral venue to set up the corporate entity that will hold the investment. The global company may be a holding company for a specific local company in the target investment country.

Another format that is quite common is where one partner is looking to develop in another location and has an opportunity to form a joint venture with a locally influential entity. One business partner thus could provide a capital investment and the other business partner could provide access to the market. A joint venture company in the local market may be considered a bias to one business partner and the global company would be preferred. The entity would also offer the variable planning structures regarding voting and nonvoting shares, the number of positions on the board, and specifically drafted articles regarding each business partner's interest.

In some cases, joint ventures provide the best opportunity to generate foreign trade income. The firm then chooses to begin a business relationship with a firm in the host country. Global joint ventures are used in a wide variety of manufacturing, mining, and service industries and frequently involve technology licensing by the U.S. firm in the joint venture.

Host country laws may require that a certain percentage (often 51 percent or more) of manufacturing or mining operations is owned by nationals of that country, thus limiting U.S. firms' local participation to minority shares of joint ventures. In addition to such legal requirements, U.S. firms may find it desirable to enter into a joint venture with a foreign firm to help spread the high costs and risks frequently associated with foreign operations.

The local partner will likely bring to the joint venture its knowledge of the customs and tastes of the people, an established distribution network, and valuable business and political contacts. Having a local partner may also lessen the foreigner image of the firm and thus provide some protection against discrimination or expropriation if conditions change.

There are some possible disadvantages to international joint ventures. A major potential drawback of joint ventures, especially in countries that limit foreign companies to minority participation, is the loss of effective managerial control. This can result in reduced profits, increased operating costs, inferior product quality, exposure to product liability, and environmental litigation and fines. U.S. firms that wish to retain effective managerial control will find this issue an important topic in negotiations with the prospective joint venture partner and the host government.

Like technology licensing agreements, joint ventures can raise U.S. or foreign antitrust issues in certain circumstances, particularly when the prospective joint venture partners are major existing or potential competitors in the affected national markets. Firms should consider applying for an export trade certificate of review from the Department of Commerce or a business review letter from the Department of Justice when significant federal antitrust issues are raised by the proposed international joint venture.

Because of the complex legal issues frequently raised by international joint venture agreements, it is very important to seek legal advice from qualified U.S. counsel before entering into any such agreement. Furthermore, U.S. firms contemplating global joint ventures should also consider retaining experienced counsel in the host country. U.S. firms may find it very disadvantageous to rely on their potential joint venture partners to negotiate host government approvals and advise them on legal issues, for their prospective partners' interests may not always coincide with their own. Qualified foreign counsel can be very helpful in obtaining government approvals and providing ongoing advice regarding the host country's intellectual property, tax, labor, corporate, commercial, antitrust, and exchange control laws.

Logistical Options in Global Operations

Global logistics is the vital link between the firm and its markets and supply sources. It is an integral element of the firm's competitive strategy. To understand the importance and changing role of logistics in any global company, one has to determine how the company's logistics activities contribute to creating a competitive advantage. To do this, logistics should be linked to the business's strategies.

Until around the early 1980s, cost leadership was widely considered the key source of competitive advantage. Cost leadership requires vigorous cost controls over all areas of operation. It favors worker and equipment specialization to increase productivity, long production runs to minimize the downtime for machine setup, and large production scales to lower unit production costs. For low-volume and customized or semicustomized products, it seeks scale economies further upstream. It uses, to the furthest extent possible, standard parts and components that the firm holds in stock and assembles or modifies into finished products according to customer orders.

Although traditional thinking often remains in place, more and more companies are recognizing the value of logistics as a way to bring value-added products or services to their global customers. Yet, many of these firms wonder if they can afford it. As air cargo companies from Federal Express down to the smallest forwarders try to extend their services in search of more business, they are increasingly telling shippers that they cannot afford not to upgrade their transport to speedy but more expensive ocean and air service.

Still, shippers are often skeptical. They say they need stronger proof that increased logistics spending will actually help their bottom lines and bring added customer value. They seem to be saying, "If the added cost of transportation and logistics makes the total cost of our product too high, it hurts our ability to compete."

For many companies, this skepticism may be the natural result of supply chains that demand greater sophistication in manufacturers' logistics departments. Integrated carrier or traditional forwarder, transport operators have gone beyond selling shippers on mere service and price; now, they are selling strategies.

Many of those strategies, of course, depend on moving goods more rapidly. Integrated carriers have sought to "unbundle" consolidations, creating more and smaller shipments. Shippers say that puts a premium on service.

The debate over the cost and benefits of logistics strategies is taking on increasing importance as shippers and their transport providers prepare for a new generation of logistics contracts. Many of the largest shippers have already wrung what efficiencies they could by consolidating vendors and tightening supply chains.

In today's highly competitive environment, being cost-efficient is essential but not, by itself, sufficient for the firm to remain globally competitive. The global company has to develop distinctive capabilities that form its core competence. Toward this end, it may outsource some operations that tie up resources but add little to its competitiveness and then refocus these resources on enhancing its core competence. It should be ready to form strategic alliances with other firms to gain competitive logistical capabilities it does not possess and cannot justify developing on its own. It should be quick to exploit time to its advantage by responding to environmental changes before competitors can react.

The quest for cost leadership entails logistics cost minimization. After all, global logistics constitutes a major cost component. Conventional logistics strategy seeks cost trade-offs among logistics activities, e. g., higher freight cost (of faster modes of transportation) for larger cost savings in inventory and warehousing. It acknowledges the importance of superior customer service, but, in practice, it seldom pursues cost-service trade-offs. It generally assumes that logistics cost would rise faster than service improvements and the additional revenues from improved service would not justify the higher cost in most cases. It treats customer service as a constraint and strives for total cost minimization, subject to maintaining a service level comparable to its competitors.

Conventional global logistics recognizes the company only as a link in the supply chain. The conventional view on competition treats suppliers and customers as two of the five forces competing against the firm (the other forces include direct rivals, new market entrants, and substitute products). These forces would seek their gains at the company's expense.

Viewing suppliers as adversaries, the firm purchases materials and logistics services from many vendors and switches among them to gain price concessions. Theoretically, the company should get lower prices for the purchased materials and services because rival vendors compete hard for its business. Buyer-seller relationships become transaction-oriented and adversarial. Information flows between the firm and its vendors are limited. Each side is concerned that any information beyond the minimum necessary for concluding and implementing a supply agreement can be used by the other side to weaken its bargaining position.

Adversarial relationships tend to justify investments in asset-intensive logistics activities like private warehousing and transportation. By bringing these logistics activities in-house, the firm can theoretically exercise tighter controls over them and thus be assured of high service quality at a lower cost. In-house logistics capabilities also lessen the company's dependence on outside vendors and strengthen its bargaining position.

The traditional quest for cost leadership creates many hidden inefficiencies such as worker and equipment specialization that reduces operating flexibility while long production runs need large buffer stocks. Although these practices may lower direct unit costs (e.g., labor cost and capital outlays per unit of output), they also reduce market responsiveness. Lead time stretches out because long production runs cannot respond quickly to market changes. Sales forecasts far into the future become less accurate; some products pile up inventories while others experience "stockouts." Back orders and rush shipments increase. They crowd out shipping and production schedules and stretch out lead time even further, with adverse consequences on forecasting accuracy and inventories. In short, customer service suffers.

Adversarial business relationships also cause inefficiencies. They undermine quality control at supply sources and thus require quality inspection of incoming materials at points of delivery. Statistical sampling techniques are used for testing small samples of materials and to determine if an entire lot meets an acceptable quality standard. This means some defective materials can pass through the system, causing adverse effects on product quality, cost, and cycle time, and negatively impacting the customer.

Outsourcing Global Logistics

Global logistics is asset-intensive. It requires physical assets (e. g., private truck fleets and warehouses) that tie up resources but may be underutilized and thus do not necessarily give the firm any competitive global advantage. This is where the global outsourcing of operations makes strategic sense. Known as third-party logistics, outsourcing logistics services enables a firm to free up its resources so they can be better used to strengthen its core competencies. Marks & Spencer, the largest British retail chain, relies totally on outside contractors to handle the physical distribution of merchandise from its global suppliers to its local stores and customers. Its decision to use third-party logistics is motivated by a desire to devote itself to its core business. As global retailers, they have specific skills in global procurement, marketing, and selling merchandise. Why blunt their focus by encumbering the operation with technical functions in which they have no expertise.

Third-party logistics also provides other benefits, including cost reduction, improved service, increased flexibility, and access to specialized expertise and information systems. As profit-driven outsiders, third-party vendors have to compete for the company's business. Competition promotes efficiency and innovation. By serving several clients, they can also attain a critical mass that their clients individually cannot. Global logistics assets become more productive in the hands of third-party vendors. For the firm, many fixed costs become variable, enabling it to expand and contract logistics operations in response to market changes.

Gillette was a target of several hostile takeover attempts in the 1980s that prompted the company to restructure its operations, trim its workforce, and sell off underutilized assets. Two of its managers proposed outsourcing global logistics services. They went on to form INTRAL, an independent logistics management company, with Gillette as the first client. INTRAL would oversee Gillette's global logistics operations, including consolidating product requirement forecasts, planning materials orders, coordinating deliveries to distribution centers, and shipping products to Gillette affiliates worldwide. Its customer base, expanded beyond Gillette, enabled it to gain concessions from carriers that Gillette could not have gained on its own.

Smaller companies may find third-party logistics essential for keeping pace with their growth. Third-party vendors offer them logistics capabilities that smaller companies either do not have the time, resources, or experience to develop internally. The founders of E-Machines, a start-up manufacturer of large-screen computer monitors, went to a trade show to sell a few prototypes to get their business started. The demand far exceeded expectations. E-Machines received large orders it would have to fill in 90 days. As a start-up company, it had only a design team. So the company had to concentrate its limited resources in establishing manufacturing and marketing operations and in contracting out logistics services. It entered a third-party logistics arrangement with TEK Logistics Services, a vendor specializing in serving the electronics industry worldwide. The arrangement gave E-Machines immediate access to an established global logistics network, something it would have needed years and millions of dollars to develop.

Using third-party logistics does not mean downgrading the importance of global logistics and operations. The firm must retain ultimate control over major logistics decisions to ensure integration of third-party services into its logistics and competitive strategies. Marks & Spencer still holds the ultimate responsibility for managing its global logistics operations, despite its total reliance on third-party contractors. It maintains a small staff that sets the parameters for logistics operations and monitors contractors' performance.

Strategic Alliances and Global Logistics Operations

In the quest for global competitive advantage, companies need to explore strategic alliance opportunities. In an alliance, individual partners gain access to the other partner's competencies that they do not possess. They increase utilization of shared resources and attain scale economies that would otherwise be elusive to any one of them operating individually. They pool resources to lower risks when the resources required for market entry are too vast to commit to on their own. They also enjoy the benefits of coordination without the problems traditionally associated with vertical integration. Each partner focuses on just one stage of operations. This focus translates into lower overhead, leaner staff, and increased responsiveness.

An important note: Strategic alliances in global operations go beyond outsourcing. When the firm outsources, it simply "rents" its partner's global operational and logistical capabilities. On the other hand, when a firm forms a strategic alliance, its main objective is to internalize its partner's distinctive global skills. It uses the alliance to build its own competencies. Strategic alliances should therefore take place within the context of the firm's long-term strategic plan to seek dramatic improvements in its competitive global position through operational collaborations.

Global logistics alliances, or partnerships, are increasingly common. Their primary focus is on quality of service. The time when customers look for low prices and acceptable product/ service quality has passed. Today's customers demand the highest quality and reasonable prices. Consumers are much more willing to pay for convenience and time-saving as they devote more time to the core competencies. Business buyers expect supporting services to help them do more with less (e. g., lower inventories and smaller staff). Smart competitors strive to expand the scope and upgrade the levels of global logistics service to maintain customer loyalty. They realize that while perfection may be unattainable, a corporate culture based on acceptable service quality will surely lead to failures. They also understand that adversarial buyer-seller relationships undermine service quality. So they turn to global logistics partnerships for essential skills and resources that they do not possess.

Through global logistics partnerships, leading competitors can realize dramatic improvements in service quality that propel them into significantly higher levels of logistics performance. They increasingly measure logistics performance in terms not only of order lead time and service dependability but also service "process" dimensions (how logistics service is being delivered). The latter dimensions include service tangibles (appearance of facilities, equipment, and personnel), responsiveness (willingness to meet customers' special requests), assurance (ability to convey trust and confidence), and empathy (attention to individual customer's requirements). Customers define high quality as service that meets or exceeds their expectations.

The global logistics partnership between Toyota, American President Companies (APC), and Fujiki Kaiun Kaisha (FKK)—known as Value-Added Service Corporation (VASCOR)—manages shipments of imported auto parts and steel to Toyota's assembly plant in Georgetown, Kentucky. It brings together partners with complementary competencies to reach a level of logistics performance that none of them can attain individually.

FKK acts as a freight forwarder and consolidator in Japan. It brings to VASCOR its extensive knowledge of Japan's transportation system. APC is the leader in container shipping on transpacific routes and intermodal transportation in the United

States. It offers a partnership unrivaled in line-haul carriage capability. Still, APC finds it necessary to supplement its carriage capacity with services from two other shipping lines that otherwise compete with it outside the scope of the VASCOR alliance. Toyota, as a pioneer in just-in-time (JIT) manufacturing, brings to VASCOR its extensive managerial experience and know-how. JIT manufacturing is nothing new at Toyota. However, JIT manufacturing, on a massive scale, across an ocean is a much more enormous challenge than anything Toyota has experienced.

Through logistics partnerships, the firm develops distinctive skills that go beyond the scope of such alliances. VASCOR helps APC build its reputation and capability as a big-ticket logistics vendor and an intermodal carrier on a global scale. APC is ready and able to work with various carriers and service vendors to offer its customers logistics services that utilize several modes of transportation, selected for their complementary service capabilities and cost economies, under a single carrier's responsibility. In fact, since the formation of VASCOR, APC has landed a third-party contract with Ford to manage the automaker's two-way materials flows between Hermosillo, Mexico, and Detroit. Its intermodal network was originally designed to handle container traffic between the United States and the Far East, serving many Japanese automobile transplants. Its rail connections run east-west instead of north-south. This proves no obstacle. Capitalizing on its experience in collaborating with rival carriers, APC forges an alliance with four railroads (three American and one Mexican) to build the necessary rail connections. Its experience in the transborder JIT operation under VASCOR also proves to be a great asset.

Global logistics partnerships thrive on cooperation. Partners must agree on common goals, define their roles, set performance expectations, establish evaluative measurements, and specify methods of compensation. On the surface, these are also typical provisions of third-party logistics. Logistics partnerships, however, go beyond third-party relationships. Third-party logistics is an outsourcing strategy. Its continued existence is conditional on attaining predefined levels of performance and cost savings.

On the other hand, a global logistics partnership is a planned, ongoing relationship. It is built on mutual gains—each partner has needs that other partners can fill. Its continued existence is conditional on attaining mutual gains, rather than on a vendor partner's ability to meet predefined cost-performance targets.

SUMMARY

In the face of growing global competition, traditional patterns of domestic manufacturing and exporting are increasingly being replaced by global networks of operational capacity. Even if companies are not presently organized globally, they are increasingly likely to need to be able to understand and operate within the global networks established by their global customers.

The effective management of global operations involves the ability to move products and services between multicontinental locations swiftly and reliably to ensure the successful servicing of emerging global customer networks.

In today's global market the opportunity for joint-venture arrangements is increasing considerably. If one organization finds a business partner with goals that are synergistic to their own, there is an opportunity for a joint venture. For many companies, joint ventures are becoming the best way to move beyond exporting and into a larger global presence.

CHAPTER 9

GLOBAL FINANCE

W ith the rise of global economic integration over recent decades, we all now live in a new world market where cross-border trade, lending, and investment activities transmit economic growth and decline across geographic borders in a matter of hours. Driven by advances in telecommunications and information technology, global financial markets and cross-border transactions have multiplied and grown exponentially in the past few years. Billions of dollars are sent around the world with the click of a mouse, passing over geographical boundaries in milliseconds. Moreover, government foreign-exchange reserves now amount to only one or two days of transactions in the foreign-exchange markets as daily volumes for such trading now exceed annual volumes in stock markets.

We now understand how new events in the world's financial markets can and do affect the lives of billions of people every day. In the past decade we have heard so much about the new emerging global economy and the tremendous opportunities that exist in foreign markets in this, now real-time dynamic global marketplace. Businesses of all sizes, in all industries struggle to understand how this impacts where the opportunities can be found and where the threats are hiding.

All this talk has led companies to consider how these new business opportunities in faraway markets will bring them new increased sales never seen before, will insulate them from the traditional swings of business cycles, and will help them build their company's brand equity on a global scale. But threats do exist, and for a variety of reasons—trade barriers, inexperience with global trade, and financial risk—some businesses have elected to bypass global markets altogether or at least for the time being. Today, many businesses that are considering venturing deeper into new global markets logically are somewhat fearful of the many uncertainties in doing business in these foreign markets, and topping this list is the lack of expertise their companies seem to have in fully understanding global finance.

The role of financial executives is changing as it never has before. To tackle the seemingly insurmountable challenges that make up global finance, the global chief financial officer or the financial director must make the leap from mere domestic financial scorekeeper to that of the global CFO, who is an astute dealmaker, has a thorough grasp of global business operations, and possesses a keen sense of global business strategy along with a repertoire of strong international financial skills.

As the role of the new global CFO is expanding, many of these new global CFOs are moving into top leadership positions within businesses, even to the top position as presidents and chief executive officers (CEOs). This should be no surprise, given the financial intricacies that are part of everyday global business life. The greatest challenge, at the same time, is the lack of experienced financial executives with global finance experience and skills.

In this chapter we will explore what global finance is and what the new global financial executives will need to know and do to both protect and lead their companies as they steadily evolve and take their place in the new global marketplace. More-over, the role of the global CFOs in small and midsize companies will place additional stress on these financial executives, for they will be required to do comparatively much more with fewer resources than their counterparts in larger companies. All is not so bleak, however; we will help the new global CFO focus on the most critical issues and aspects of global finance and explain where the most attention should be directed. We will also attempt to provide key insights and helpful suggestions about potential new ideas and tools that can ease some of the pressures along the way. First, let's take a look at what global finance is and how global business is impacting the whole area of finance, particularly for small and midsize companies.

WHAT IS GLOBAL FINANCE?

Global finance is much more than cashing international letters of credit or having an offshore bank account or a trading company in a third country. Global finance is taking full advantage of swings in the world's financial markets by fully integrating institutions on a global, regional, or local level to ensure the fluidity and free flow of capital. Global finance leverages the different capabilities of particular financial partners, i.e., banks, other financial institutions, governments, and venture capitalists.

Global finance entails the upkeep of a wide reach in both primary and secondary markets; leveraging the strength of different financial relationships; forming alliance relationships and joint ventures with suppliers, governments, and distributors; and, assuring fluidity by keeping financial options from both an inflow and outflow perspective. Companies that truly grasp the intricacies of global finance possess all of the following:

- Working knowledge of the roles banks serve in the global marketplace

- Understanding of the different payment methods used in international business, including the advantages and disadvantages of each method

- Recognition of the reality of political risk and how to evaluate and manage political risk

- Sense of the implications of global currency exchange rates and their impact on global business transactions

- Feel for hedging techniques used in international monetary exchanges

- In-depth comprehension of all forms of payment used in international trade

- Firm grasp of the major financing alternatives open to companies conducting global business

- Keen understanding of nontraditional payment schemes and other customary and traditional international practices, irrespective of whether the global company will engage in these practices

- Awareness of the portfolio of services typically offered by global nonbank financial institutions

Global finance is continuing to evolve along with the new global economy. As can be seen by the previous list, global finance encompasses a wide and diverse range of issues within a company. Moreover, the issues that are the responsibility of the global CFO are some of the most complex in the company. Even the most cogent, effective business strategies can be easily undermined by one of the many thorny issues that can arise in the area of global finance. For example, in many markets that still have a comprehensive set of customs and import duty taxes and fees that must be paid, a misfiled document or an improperly filed tax return could make the difference between profit or loss in that company's business in a particular market.

In global business, the risks are great if anything is left to chance or to ignorance. More than any other discipline with the global company, the global finance executive must protect and secure the company from the many seen and unseen traps that await companies when doing business in markets globally.

GLOBAL BUSINESS FINANCE ISSUES

Skilled financial executives are key to a company's success when venturing into foreign markets in the new global economy, regardless of company size, but especially for the small or midsize company. As companies begin to do business requiring them to cross more borders, the complexity of their international operations increases. Managing this complexity goes well beyond simple finance management and accounting practices. Companies need expert global finance executives who are capable of creating innovative financial solutions that solve complicated and tedious international business issues and who can provide overall guidance to other functional executives within these same companies.

Global company CFOs and other global finance executives must continue to evaluate what is vital to determine whether the current and future needs of the global business are being met. To the extent possible, global finance professionals must consider what can and should be done in-house as well as what assistance they may require from professional services firms with experiences from other clients and diverse regions of the world. When determining the global business operational needs of the company, global finance executives have the following responsibilities:

- Provide assurances to management, corporate directors, investors, lenders, and others on the reliability of financial and nonfinancial information, business processes and controls, regulatory compliance, and information used in strategic transactions.

- Possess the appropriate tools and resources to analyze the global business objectives, operations, and markets.

- Help internal clients (functional departments) develop customer, supply chain, e-business, asset-optimization, and management solutions; strategy and planning tactics; and change-enabling guidance.

- Assist in creating, enhancing, and maximizing enterprise value by originating and executing transactions such as mergers, acquisitions, and divestitures. Facilitate access to capital markets, devise strategies to optimize the value of real estate assets, and develop restructuring programs.

- Help internal clients (functional departments) focus on the business transformation required by e-business in strategy, customer interaction, business models, and their entire business operation.

- Help internal clients (functional departments) realize the value of their people by developing unique solutions to attract, manage, and retain employees while offering services in the areas of compensation and equity incentives, international employment solutions, HR management, and in retirement, actuarial, and benefits consulting.

- Understand where the global business should be investing heavily, e.g., research and development of innovative global business solutions that fit the company's vision.

- Assist in designing, implementing, and operating certain finance and accounting business processes to enable internal clients (functional departments) to sharpen their strategic business focus to improve the performance of these essential, but noncore, business elements.

- Help internal clients (functional departments) understand and manage business risks that can affect performance and financial results, including risks relating to business processes, technology, regulatory compliance, government contracting, fraud, and treasury and trading activities.

- Maximize the global business's value by identifying and implementing comprehensive strategies for corporate, international, indirect, and local taxes.

DEVELOPING A GLOBAL FINANCE STRATEGY

It's easy for small and midsize businesses to view global trade as an insurmountable challenge because of the many business risks involved—most of them centering on financial risks. In many markets, for example, accurate credit information on potential customers, suppliers, and other trading partners is difficult to obtain, and credit analysis is further complicated by differences in accounting standards and procedures. Foreign banking systems can present further obstacles—everything from forward and back valuing on payment instruments, to foreign-exchange transaction exposure, to delays in clearing international funds. Furthermore, traditional trade finance tools such as bank letters of credit and credit insurance can be costly to use and difficult to manage. Most important, companies engaging in global business transactions must weigh carefully the financial risks of offering potential customers, suppliers and other trading partners the open account terms they require, especially in countries whose legal systems unreasonably protect domestic debtors from their foreign creditors.

At the same time, in today's new global business environment, maintaining solely a domestic focus in a company's business can be every bit as risky, particularly as competitors gain strength by tapping into global markets, which include everyone's own domestic markets. Consequently, in virtually all industries, more and more companies are committing themselves to doing global business and making it work.

A principal concern for suppliers is to ensure that payment will be made in full and on time. Global customers have their own concerns, including uncertainties that the goods ordered would meet the necessary specifications or arrive in a timely manner. As a result, terms of payment must be agreed on in advance in a manner satisfactory to both parties.

PAYMENT METHODS OF GLOBAL FINANCE

The payment method used can significantly affect the financial risk of a particular business strategy. In general, the more generous the sales terms are to a global customer, the greater the risk to the seller. The primary methods of payment for international transactions, ranked in order of most secure to least secure, include:

- Payment in advance

- Letters of credit (LC)

- Documentary collections (drafts)

- Consignment

- Open account

Payment in Advance

Paying in advance is often too expensive and risky for customers. Yet, this method of payment is not uncommon. Requiring full payment in advance may cause lost sales to a foreign (or even another domestic) competitor who is able to offer more attractive payment terms. In some cases, however, where the manufacturing process is specialized, lengthy, or capital-intensive, it may be reasonable to insist on partial payment in advance, or on progress payments.

Letters of Credit (LC)

A letter of credit (LC) is an internationally recognized instrument issued by a bank on behalf of its client, the purchaser. The letter of credit actually represents the bank's guarantee to pay the seller, provided the conditions specified on it are fulfilled. Of course, the purchaser pays its bank a fee to render this service.

With a letter of credit, the seller relies on the creditworthiness of the bank, which is normally more reliable than that of the purchaser. It is also easier to verify by the seller's bank. Moreover, this vehicle can be structured to protect the purchaser because no payment obligation arises until the goods have been satisfactorily delivered as promised.

The conditions of the letter of credit are spelled out in the document itself. When the conditions of delivery have been satisfied (usually by the documented, satisfactory, and timely delivery of the goods), the purchaser's bank makes the required payment directly to the seller's bank in accordance with the terms of payment (in 15, 30, 60, or 90 days, whichever is specified).

The greatest degree of protection is afforded to the seller when the letter of credit has been issued by the buyer's bank and confirmed by the seller's bank. Letters of credit may be utilized for one-time transactions, or they can cover multishipments, depending on what is agreed between the parties.

The typical process for a letter of credit is as follows:

Buyer	Seller
Agrees to buy product.	Agrees to ship goods if LC is opened.
	LC assures payment if proper documents are presented.
Requests bank to issue LC.	Ships goods and submits shipping documents to bank for payment.
Verifies documents for compliance.	
Payment is made immediately or on maturity of accepted draft.	Payment is made when documents received or accepted.

Documentary Collection (Drafts)

Documentary collections involve the use of a draft, drawn by the seller on the buyer, requiring the buyer to pay the face amount either on sight (sight draft) or on a specified date in the future (time draft). The draft is an unconditional order to make such payment in accordance with its terms, which specify the documents needed before title to the goods will be passed.

Because title to the goods does not pass until the draft is paid or accepted, both the buyer and seller are protected. If the buyer defaults on payment of the draft, however, the seller may have to pursue collection through the courts (or possibly, by arbitration, if such had been agreed on between the parties). The use of drafts involves a certain level of risk, but they are less expensive for the purchaser than letters of credit.

The typical process for a documentary collections (draft) is as follows:

Buyer	Seller
	Agrees to be paid via documentary collection.
Agrees to buy products	Ships goods and submits shipping documents to bank for collection or acceptance.
Documents released to buyer against payment or acceptance.	Seller receives payment on sight on acceptance.

Consignment

When goods are sold subject to consignment, the supplier receives no money until the purchaser has sold the goods. Until such time as all the purchase conditions are satisfied, title to the goods remains with the supplier. As a practical matter, consignment is very risky. Generally, there is no way to predict how long it might take to sell the goods; moreover, if they are never sold, the supplier would have to pay the costs of recovering them from the foreign consignee.

Open Account

An open-account transaction means that the goods are manufactured and delivered before payment is required (for example, payment could be due 14, 30, or 60 days following shipment or delivery). In the United States, sales are likely to be made on an open-account basis if the manufacturer has been dealing with the buyer over a long period of time and has established a secure working relationship. In global business transactions, this method of payment cannot be used safely unless the buyer is creditworthy and the country of destination is politically and economically stable. In certain instances, however, it might be possible to discount open accounts receivable with a factoring company or other financial institution.

An experienced global firm extends credit cautiously. It evaluates new customers with care and continuously monitors older accounts. This firm may wisely decide to decline a customer's request for open-account credit if the risk is too great and propose instead payment on delivery terms through a documentary sight draft or irrevocable confirmed letter of credit or even payment in advance. On the other hand, for a fully creditworthy customer, the experienced firm may decide to allow a month or two to pay, perhaps even on open account.

The drawback to cash in advance is that customers almost everywhere in the world have become accustomed to the flexibility and convenience of open-account relationships and may typically object to making payment before delivery. Another well-established option, bank letters of credit, are effective and relatively convenient for the seller, but they are growing unpopular with buyers because they place a significant administrative and financial burden on the buyer to open, maintain, and pay the expenses associated with the LC. LCs also may limit the buyer's financial flexibility by tying up valuable credit lines that could be used for other purposes. In addition, confirmations for the receipt of goods or payments are not always readily available for all banks around the world, and disputes can be difficult and costly to resolve. Another option, credit insurance, usually does not provide full coverage to the seller, and its deductible and/or coinsurance payments may expose global sellers to additional credit risks. Furthermore, using credit insurance does provide limited collection support, but it typically requires the selling company to perform its own credit investigations. This places a large burden on the small or midsize companies selling their products and services in foreign markets to prove their claims.

In the end, global financial executives must wrestle with a number of key issues to protect their companies, while at the same time, ease the way for their companies to take advantage of the new business opportunities available in new foreign markets.

UNDERSTANDING THE DOMESTIC BANKING ENVIRONMENT

In the United States, most small firms turn first to their local banks for global finance assistance. During the past decade, however, many banks have decided not to focus on global business financing.

The banks' reasons for doing so have varied: Many cut their international operations because of the huge losses they incurred on overseas debt; others may have chosen to concentrate on more lucrative lines of business, such as home equity loans or mergers and acquisitions.

Consequently, during the 1980s, global finance expertise in many U.S. banks deteriorated. Even today, most small banks do not retain any staff with expertise in global trade. This help is still available, so small businesses must be extremely persistent and tenacious in locating it. For example, if a loan officer is unwilling to work with his or her bank's international staff (or the bank is unwilling to work with a correspondent), companies should consider establishing a second banking relationship or, if necessary, moving all their accounts to a more aggressive lender. Don't be afraid to shop.

Because many global companies face difficulties when seeking financing, financial arrangements must be made in advance. To find a lender willing to consider such a request, the borrower must ensure that the purpose of the loan makes sense for the business, and that the request is a reasonable amount.

It is also important to note the difference between general working capital financing and trade financing. A firm's ability to qualify for general working capital financing depends on, among other things, the strength of its balance sheet and its prospects for generating sufficient earnings over the life of a loan to repay it. Trade finance, on the other hand, generally refers to financing individual transactions (or a series of like transactions). In addition, trade finance loans are often self-liquidating, that is, the lending bank stipulates that all sales proceeds are to be collected by it, and then it applies the proceeds to pay down the loan. The remainder is credited to the account of the borrower.

Lenders who may otherwise have reached their lending limits for such businesses may nevertheless finance global sales, if the lenders are assured that the loan proceeds will be used solely for preexport production and that any sale proceeds will first be collected by them before the balance is passed on to the exporter. Given the extent of control lenders can exercise over such transactions and the existence of guaranteed payment mechanisms unique to—or established for—global trade, trade finance can be less risky for lenders than general working capital loans.

NONBANK GLOBAL FINANCE SOURCES

Beyond banks, several private sources of capital exist for companies looking to expand their global presence.

Private Trade Finance Companies

Private trade finance companies are becoming increasingly more commonplace. They utilize a variety of financing techniques in return for fees, commissions, or participation in the transactions or combinations of any of these. International trade associations, such as District Export Councils that exist in every state, can assist in locating a private trade finance company.

Export Trading Companies (ETCs) and Export Management Companies (EMCs)

Both export trading companies (ETCs) and export management companies (EMCs) provide varying ranges of services, including global market research and overseas marketing, insurance, legal assistance, product design, transportation, foreign order processing, warehousing, overseas distribution, foreign exchange, and even taking title to a supplier's goods.

Factoring Houses

Factoring houses, also called factors, purchase global receivables on a discounted basis. Using factors can enable a company to receive immediate payment for goods while at the same time alleviating the hassles associated with overseas collections.

Factors purchase global receivables for a percentage fee at 2 percent to 7 percent below the invoice value, depending on the market and type of buyer. The percentage rate depends on whether the factor purchases the receivables on a recourse or nonrecourse basis. In the case of a nonrecourse purchase, the supplier is not bound to repay the factoring house if the foreign buyer defaults or other collection problems arise. Therefore, the percentage charge will be greater with nonrecourse purchases.

Forfeiting Houses

Similar to factoring, suppliers relinquish their rights to future payment in return for immediate cash. Where a debt obligation exists between the parties, it is sold to a third party on a nonrecourse basis, but is guaranteed by an intermediary bank.

One U.S.-based company that used forfeiting found the benefits substantial: Ed Lamb, president of Custom Die and Insert of

Lafayette, Louisiana, was able to sell a 180-day letter of credit through a forfeiting house and got paid 178 days sooner. Forfeiting enabled Custom Die and Insert to consummate a $12.3 million order to its distributor in the Middle East.

ASSESSING GLOBAL POLITICAL RISK

As with all global business activity, political risk and its consequential impact on business must be assessed and balanced against the gains associated with these potential activities. The definition of an acceptable level of risk will vary from company to company. And, as investment advertisements will tell you, the past is not a reliable guide to the future. In addition, the global business world is becoming more risky.

Increasingly, successful global companies are asking senior financial managers to focus exclusively on the link between global strategy and risk management. The two are inextricably linked. Increased risk is associated with doing global business and it is largely up to the new global finance executives to ensure such risks are minimized while allowing the company to still take advantage of the staggering potential offered by the new global marketplace.

As we observed in our previous book, ascertained risk is managed risk. Because of the speed at which global financial events can seemingly spin out of control, companies have to think the unthinkable and then find ways of managing it. The process of thinking the unthinkable forces the reappraisal of assumptions underlying every aspect of the global finance area in question.

Global finance executives can be both catalysts and facilitators in helping their companies prevent, or at least minimize, such things as well as prepare their companies to best handle any such eventualities that are certain to occur.

ASSESSING FOREIGN CURRENCY EXPOSURE: HEDGING

To best manage their foreign currency exposures, companies ideally need to know why and when current and future financial market crises and economic downturns will spread from one country to another. They can then develop a monitoring system that helps them recognize when any changes or shifts begin to occur.

An economic slowdown in one market leads to lower exports for neighboring markets, eventually slowing their economies as well. These slowing economies, in turn, further reduce the demand for the first market's exports, exerting more downward pressure on that economy, and so forth, with a cascading effect.

Consequently, cross-border economic problems are likely to be stronger for markets that trade a great deal with each other, like Mexico and the United States, or Argentina and Brazil, or Germany and Russia. If a market tries to counteract declining exports with price reductions using mechanisms such as currency devaluation, its trading partners may do the same to negate its price advantage. Thus, as an economy and the international value of its currency deteriorate, a market is no longer a good customer for its neighbor's exports (in fact, because of the declining value of its currency, it is ready, willing, and able to export more to these neighboring markets).

These currency and economic effects interact to reinforce the negative impacts on a country's trade balances and economic prospects. Logically, this will increase the currency risk to any company conducting business in that market or in any market(s) within any given region.

The global financial executive must maintain a watchful eye on any trends or hints of such potential instabilities around the world and assess when and to what extent such financial exposure from currency fluctuations may occur.

For many companies, the word *hedging* conjures up thoughts of wild speculation and overnight catastrophes. Some companies, as a matter of policy, forgo hedging altogether, often with the explanation that the kind of selective hedging many companies use is only a small step removed from a spin on the roulette wheel. Using the option to hedge against global finance risks might be the best thing from a long-term, cash-flow perspective, but in the short term, it may mean accepting (and having to explain) volatile earnings.

For many, if a company has an exposure and decides not to manage it, that is speculation. When a company assumes an exposure because of a conscious decision, then it's not speculating, it's taking a financial position based on some fundamental analysis. Still, many companies wrongly keep hedging out of their global finance strategy. Nevertheless, currency, credit, and political risk are major parts of global business, and the more a company understands the dynamics, the better equipped it is to handle volatility.

MONITORING THE DOLLAR

A company with a well-run global finance strategy is going to understand its exposures to a relatively weak or strong dollar and consistently monitor them. For U.S. companies or for companies doing business in the United States, monitoring the relative strength or weakness of the U.S. dollar is fundamental to a company's global finance strategy. The same holds true, in a reciprocal way, for European and Japanese companies with the Euro and the yen, respectively.

When the U.S. dollar is strong, U.S. companies typically have to pursue cost-cutting measures and perhaps accept lower profit margins because it takes more Euros, yens, or pesos to buy dollars; products manufactured in the United States are now more expensive in foreign currency terms, even if their price in dollars remains constant.

A strong U.S. dollar also means foreign currency revenues are worth less in U.S. dollar terms. This can create a distortion between business performance and reported financial results. For example, in 1999, Ford sold more cars in Europe than the previous year, but those sales were worth fewer dollars. Coke sold more cola during that same time, but its stock lost its fizz when the company was forced to announce disappointing financial results blamed almost exclusively on the strong dollar. And during the same period, Johnson & Johnson announced the strong dollar had cost it 9 percent of its international revenues, because of foreign-exchange adjustments.

Global companies face exposures to currency, interest rates, credit, political and other international business risks. When doing business outside the United States, like it or not, companies are exposed to currency fluctuations and credit losses. Some choose to deny it. Others choose to accept it and try to manage the risk.

To say, however, that even the most successful companies will never suffer currency or credit losses is not true. Even the smartest firms will occasionally get burned. Nothing risked; nothing gained. The difference is that companies that succeed in the global finance strategy are rarely, if ever, surprised.

Whether the company is a buyer or a seller, foreign-exchange movements will invariably impact the financial performance of its business. To the extent possible, it is up to the global CFO to monitor and develop strategies utilizing unavoidable currency fluctuations in the world's currencies to their company's advantage.

SUMMARY

Aspiring global company CEOs must carefully reconsider the current functions of all departments and the roles their top executives play. They must then develop strategies to transition key members of their organizations, beginning with themselves and top executives, to lead their companies in finding ways to better leverage the inevitable phases of global manifest destiny. And, leading these companies into the new borderless economy must include the new global CFO as a key member of the global executive management team.

Unlike traditional finance and CFOs of the past, the new global finance function is being asked to do much more, and the new CFO must step out of his or her office and into an entirely new role: global CFO. He or she must perform as a strategic partner with other high-ranking senior executives from business operations across the company. Moreover, the new global finance function and global CFO will now be called on to spend more time with the CEO and other key business executives on strategic activities such as mergers and acquisitions and strategic planning—now critical in developing and expanding business globally.

Many finance executives today realize the traditional business model is becoming obsolete in the new borderless economy. No longer is the finance department's role narrowly limited to securing funding for the CEO's proposed business initiatives, turning out financial statements on demand, scrutinizing corporate spending, and otherwise keeping busy with routine and mundane transaction processing.

The new global CEOs now expect finance to help them manage the dramatic changes brought about by an increasingly global business environment. Global finance's new mission involves partnerships. Global finance professionals must bring their inherent analytical capability to bear on the problems and decision-making challenges of local operating managers on the front lines in markets throughout the world.

Succeeding in this new and demanding partnership will not be easy, as global finance must shift its focus from performing traditional tasks to new strategic activities with exponentially higher potential payoffs for their enterprises. Global finance also must manage more than just risk exposure in the financial markets. It must now focus on a wider range of business exposure and work to develop strategies that minimize risks while exploiting emerging opportunities in far-flung markets.

Global finance executives worldwide now have a unique opportunity to step outside their traditional functional boundaries to assist boards of directors and CEOs with achieving strategic objectives, particularly those objectives related to worldwide business growth. As customers demand greater value for their money and shareholders seek ever-higher financial performance, new business opportunities on the global frontier may provide the answer for beleaguered CEOs.

No company today can tolerate a finance department stuck in the past. Moreover, companies needing to compete globally cannot afford CFOs not deeply committed to being active participants in global business strategy development and implementation. Global business development executives need to enter new foreign markets with knowledgeable and globally savvy finance leaders who can quickly set up new, market-appropriate systems and processes for managing working capital and analyzing profitability by market segment and distribution channel. Company sales executives need insights into competitors' costs that only a true global finance department can provide. And lastly, to make the best decisions possible on large capital investments, senior executives need direction on how different businesses and operations can create and sustain increasing demands for higher shareholder value.

Such a dramatic transformation can only begin if the needs of the new global company are realized. If today's finance departments and those individuals leading them are to become radically more effective and directly engaged in securing the company's new global growth objectives, global finance and global CFOs must change the fundamental ways they think and how they relate to virtually every aspect of the new global organization.

CHAPTER 10

LEVERAGING GLOBAL MANIFEST DESTINY

The economic integration of humankind has been a march throughout recorded history. Punctuated by periods of equilibrium, global manifest destiny, the inevitability of all of the world's citizens to be brought together by economic means, has at times expanded rapidly across the planet and at other moments retrenched itself, seemingly waiting for another day. The breakneck pace of recent events has caused a complete reevaluation of all our old beliefs and explanations. Asia's meteoric rise and apparent overnight collapse seems at times inexplicable, more for our failure to anticipate it rather than it actually occurring. America's unimpeded economic expansion for more than a decade seems to defy the conventional models. China's rise as a global superpower appears on the horizon like a hazy sunrise, easy to see but difficult to define.

Experts try to rationalize such occurrences using popular but failed paradigms like *globalization* and *global economy*. Such terms are more often than not used to explain, justify, permit, and endorse the actions of one particular group against another.

The financial markets tell us that because of globalization, seemingly stable economies and companies can be brought down to their knees almost overnight—workers are bankrupted; national banks looted; currencies devalued; and companies degraded. The absurd preoccupation with instant gratification has become a "day-trading mentality": terribly shortsighted and inherently dangerous for government and business leaders alike. Yet, no models currently exist to truly explain how this happens.

There is hope, however, and global manifest destiny holds the promise. By recognizing, embracing, and assimilating global manifest destiny as part of the very fabric of their organizations, forward-thinking leaders will undoubtedly be the ones who benefit from the inevitable economic integration of humankind. Those who fail to do so will eventually be disregarded and easily forgotten.

For the vast majority of U.S. firms, fully leveraging global manifest destiny mandates that they must go beyond simple exporting. Companies of every size in every industry must at least recognize the inevitability of global economic integration and prepare their future business strategies accordingly. For those companies who choose to do nothing in the face of global manifest destiny, they will be certain to face an even greater onslaught of global competition as they fight to hold on to their niche market.

For companies that desire only to expand the export facet of their business, they will need to realize that companies in emerging markets will become stronger adversaries over the long-term.

For those firms that desire to go beyond and establish a strong, long-term global presence, they will have to restructure and retool their organizations based on much of what we have presented in this book.

The global companies of the future will be seamless and transparent organizations that possess the critical ability to adapt to an ever-changing global business landscape. They will embody cultures and processes that will keep them in front of any changes or shifts in the global economy.

APPENDIX A

INTERNET RESOURCE GUIDE

W e recommend the following Internet Web sites that relate to the seven global competencies for growing your business worldwide.

The lists are invariably eclectic and are limited because of space. If you have any comments or suggestions for future editions on this topic, please send them to *info@globalmanifestdestiny.com*.

Global Culture

www.globalmanifestdestiny.com
Premier site providing breaking global business news

www.adecco.com
Job-finding site from one of the world's largest recruitment companies

www.africanews.org
Africa News Online, with wide geographical and topical coverage

www.arabia.com
Arabia Online, including current affairs, business news, and cultural coverage from the Arab world

www.brazzil.com
Monthly Brazilian magazine focusing on business and current affairs

www.business-times.asia1.com.sg
Business Times of Singapore, a leading business daily with coverage throughout Southeast Asia

www.careers.wsj.com
Wall Street Journal's Career Section

www.emdsnet.com
Global recruitment services from EMDS, a global consultancy

www.european-voice.com
A weekly newspaper on EU affairs, published by The Economist Group

www.ft.com
The *Financial Times*, an excellent source for global business news

www.iht.com
The *International Herald Tribune*

www.japantimes.co.jp
The *Japan Times*

www.jobasia.com
Large Asian recruitment site

www.latpro.com
Latin American professional recruitment site, for Spanish and Portuguese speakers

www.mg.co.za
Pan-African business encyclopedia

www.moscowtimes.ru
The *Moscow Times*

www.scmp.com
The daily *South China Morning Post*, including extensive news coverage of Hong Kong and China

www.smh.com.au
The *Sydney Morning Herald*

www.timesofindia.com
The *Times of India*

Global Marketing

www.adage.com
Advertising Age, a worldwide marketing and advertising industry newsletter

www.arts.gla.ac.uk
This unit at Glasgow University provides information services on Central and Eastern Europe

www.asia-pacific.com
Strategic business information on the Asia-Pacific with news, analysis, data, books, journals, experts, and other resources

www.business-spain.com

Business Spain covers market sectors, companies, economy, etc.

www.countrywatch.com

Economic, business, geographic, and other information about 191 countries. Fee for expanded services

www.doingbusinessin.com

Quick overviews of the investment climate, taxation, forms of business organization, and business and accounting practices in 141 countries

www.eiu.com

The Economist Intelligence Unit makes its well-respected country reports available

www.emerging-markets.com

Market research service specializing in power, energy, telecoms, and utilities markets of Latin America, Asia, and Eastern Europe

www.export.gov.il

Information on the economy, doing business in Israel, directory of Israeli exporters, etc.

www.export-japan.com

Portal site for market research in Japan

www.ghana.gov.gh

A guide provided by the government of Ghana that presents the business environment in Ghana

www.gmmso.com

Site that provides customized online international market analysis reports for diverse industries and products

www.ihk.de
Site of the German Chamber of Commerce

www.mecon.ar
Gives overviews of some industry sectors, together with background information on Argentinian investment law, taxation

www.odci.gov/cia
The *CIA World Factbook* is available at the Central Intelligence Agency site at countries. Subscriber-only service (corporate): 14-day trial available. Worldwide.

www.strategis.ic.gc.ca
Industry Canada includes monthly economic indicators, provincial overviews (business activity and prospects), statistical industry overviews, licensable technology opportunities, import/export data, patent database, detailed information on key industry sectors

www.thomasregister.com
Searchable database of brand names, products, and services from the *Thomas Register of American Manufacturers*

www.trace-sc.com
Mexico index of about 10,000 links, including a directory of company sites, links to statistics on trade and economics, yellow pages directory, news links

www.ucis.pitt.edu
Links to information in all areas of east and central European study, including business and economics sources

www.ultrachina.com/english
Market research for doing business with China

www.worldskip.com
Information about markets and local news from most countries

www.wk.or.at
Statistics on Austrian exports, forthcoming events, data on import duties, information on a very wide range of business opportunities.

Global Account Management Programs

www.accountmanagementcenter.com
A Key Account Management spin-off of the University of St. Gallen

www.caslione.com
Articles, comments, and insights from one of the authors with regard to global account management programs

www.kamcity.com
The original newsletter for key account managers

www.nams.org
The Strategic Account Management Association

www.salesandmarketing.com
A magazine for executives who work in strategic accounts management

www.sales-research-trust.org
A not-for-profit providing a focus for collaboration between managers and academics in the area of strategic customer account management

www.smsweb.org
Brings together the practice and scholarship of strategic account management

Global Customer Service

www.asponline.com
An international organization dedicated to the advancement of the technical support profession

www.callcenterdepot.com
A one-stop online for call center resources

www.crmmag.com
Monthly magazine, Web site

www.customersupport.org
A nonprofit alliance of leading technology companies working together to solve customer service challenges

www.customersupportmgmt.com
Publication dedicated to customer service support

www.icsa.com
Organization for the customer service industry

www.smiweb.com
Customer service publications and conferences

Global E-business

www.asiacommerce.com
A consortium of Asia Business-to-Business e-Commerce service providers

www.becrc.com

The ECRC program mission is to improve U.S. industry's and government's global competitiveness by promoting awareness and implementation of electronic commerce technologies and practices

www.e-business.pwcglobal.com

PricewaterhouseCoopers's e-business site

www.herring.com

Business news, technology, and research for investors and consumers

www.thestandard.net

News, features, and statistics about the Internet economy

Global Procurement

www.assetline.com

Auction for construction, industrial, manufacturing, and transportation equipment

www.b2business.net

Links to e-marketplaces

www.bidtheworld.com

Business-to-business site for conducting auctions of business purchase orders, requests for prices, and contracts to suppliers worldwide

www.bizbuyer.com

A system that sends requests for purchases to registered sellers of many goods and services

www.bizsurplus.com

Auctions of new and used surplus MRO inventory, safety supplies, tools, and equipment

www.bliquid.com

Online industrial auction where businesses contact each other to buy and sell surplus and used industrial equipment and supplies

www.globalsources.com

Product and trade information and links for volume buyers of consumer, business, and industrial goods

www.meetchina.com

Auctions for Chinese-made products

www.metalsite.com

Site that enables immediate purchase of steel and steel products

www.procurenet.com

Web-based procurement system that creates a custom-built catalog of a company's top suppliers

www.purchasepro.com

A standard platform for small business and corporate purchasing departments to buy and sell products in secure, online open and private marketplaces

www.purchasingsupersite.com

A purchasing portal aimed at four primary sector groups: manufacturing, services, government, and academia

www.tradequote.com

Allows manufacturers and producers from more than 600 industries to receive detailed requests for price quotes from purchasers around the world

Global Operations

www.asiaship.com
Directory of shipping companies and logistics service providers in Asia

www.attorneyfind.com
Database of attorneys searchable by specialty and location

www.cargo-online.com
A central database of worldwide available air charter capacity and requirements

www.cargonow.com
Portal site and marketplace for companies in the transportation industry as well as companies that purchase transportation services

www.cargoweb.com
Complete and free information service for the transportation and logistics industries. Includes news, directories, and country and industry information

www.containershipping.com
Links to sources of container shipping news, market reports, statistics, analysis, directories, guides, and more

www.freightforwarders.org
Directory of freight services worldwide

www.freightworld.com
More than 3,500 links to trade and logistics-related sites

www.interleges.com
An international association of independent law firms, with offices across the countries of the European Union, Eastern Europe, North America, the Middle East, and in other key commercial regions of the world

www.maerskline.com
Maersk Line's site, including booking and shipment tracking

www.mcb.co.uk/ijpdlm.htm
International Journal of Physical Distribution and Logistics Management provides wide and deep coverage of key issues and the latest developments in distribution and logistics management

www.mcb.co.uk/scm.htm
Supply Chain Management Journal, covering aspects of marketing, logistics and information technology, economics, management, and organizational behavior in relation to the operation of supply chains in all sectors

www.mmdonline.com
Material, Management and Distribution Magazine provides a solution-oriented editorial approach to the movement, storage, and control of materials, products, and information

www.mypid.com
The Marine Yellow Pages, a search engine of more than 21,000 companies

www.ponl.com
Site for P&O Nedlloyd

www.smlawpub.co.uk
This annual international directory provides information on approximately 650 law firms and chambers throughout the world, covering nearly 250 countries

www.supplylinks.com
Global supply chain network that links customers to multiple transportation modes and service providers through a single platform

www.synchronetmarine.com
Site that matches empty containers with shippers and shipping companies worldwide

www.uschinalaw.com
Network of law firms involved in the United States and China

www.winsnykline.com
NYK's site, including booking and shipment tracking

www.wsdonline.com
Database with details of more than 45,000 marine-based companies

www.worldtariff.com
Publication of customs duty and tax information for all customs areas worldwide

Global Finance

www.acca-usa.org
Association of Chartered Certified Accountants site, listing many finance and accounting resources

www.adr.com

A directory of American depository receipts or non-U.S. companies that trade in the U.S. stock market. Price history graph, balance sheet, etc., and links to other company data. Information from J.P. Morgan and the Carson Group Inc. Worldwide

www.asx.com.au

Australian Stock Exchange

www.bfanet.com

Key information from annual reports of South African public companies (key financials, personnel, company ownership, chairman's statement, graphs)

www.bis.org

The Bank for International Settlements, the central bank of central banks

www.bloomberg.com

Financial market updates and analysis

www.bog.frb.fed.us

The Federal Reserve

www.boj.or.jp/en

The Bank of Japan

www.bundesbank.de

The Bundesbank

www.bvdep.com

Financial data on 200,000 European companies, available on pay-per-use basis

www.cerved.com
Priced service, requiring registration. Financials of the five million companies registered with Italian Chambers of Commerce (the SANI database)

www.ebr.org
Site of the European Union project to give access to information filed on all EU companies through a common interface

www.ecb.int
The European Central Bank

www.fin-info.com
Information (news, stock prices) for Canadian-listed companies

www.fnet.de
News stories (about companies and stock exchanges in Europe); prices from the German stock exchanges; chart of DAX

www.globalfindata.com
Current and historical financial data

www.globalregister.co.nz
New Zealand companies section has information (press releases, annual reports with financials, share movement) for selected industries

www.hedgeindex.com
Statistical database on hedge fund performance

www.hoovers.com
Global company directory with financial data, company news, and links

www.ifc.org
The International Finance Organization

www.imf.org
The International Monetary Fund

www.kreller.com
Credit-rating reports, country-risk reports with worldwide financials

www.latinfinance.com
A monthly magazine of investment news from Latin America

www.moodys.com
Describes their worldwide credit research services

www.rmonline.com
The Raymond Morris Group offers various reports, some online and some offline, on UK companies, e.g., financials, credit check, trademark. Is also launching U.S. private company search service

www.securities.com
Offers business information (news, company financial statements, stock quotes, analyst reports, market research, etc.) concentrating on Central and Eastern Europe, Latin America, and other emerging markets

www.thestreet.com
Detailed reports and analysis from Wall Street

www.worldbank.org
The World Bank

www.wto.org
The World Trade Organization

APPENDIX B

MULTILATERAL AND REGIONAL DEVELOPMENT BANKS AND ORGANIZATIONS

L oosely associated with the United Nations are the World Bank and the International Monetary Fund, two large, powerful organizations whose purpose is to assist in development in the less modern areas of the world. In addition, there are four regional development organizations with similar objectives.

As possible financing sources, directly or indirectly, the international development banks through their many projects also offer numerous supply opportunities for equipment manufacturers, engineers, consultants, construction firms, and similar businesses. The banks produce publications indicating their procurement needs.

The World Bank
1818 H Street, NW
Washington, DC 20433
USA
Telephone: 202-477-1234
Fax: 202-477-6391

The primary goal of the World Bank and its affiliates is to raise the standard of living in developing countries. The bank finances a broad range of capital infrastructure projects but particularly focuses on investments that improve the quality of life of whole populations. It also promotes economic development and structural reform in the countries in which it is involved. There are two parts of the bank: the International Bank for Reconstruction and Development (IBRD) and the International Development Association (IDA). Both lend funds, give advice, and try to get investments moving, with the IDA specifically concentrating on the poorer countries and providing easier financial terms. An affiliate—the International Finance Corporation—relates directly to the private sector. It invests its own funds as well as seeks out other monies for commercial enterprises. Another affiliate is the Multilateral Investment Guarantee Agency, which seeks to protect the investor from political risks.

The World Bank will speak with you and may produce or lead you to your needed financing. The bank has offices throughout the world, but Washington, D.C., is the location of its world headquarters. The bank also publishes the *International Business Opportunities Service,* to which you can subscribe by contacting World Bank Publications at Room T8094 at the above address, or by calling, in the United States, 202-473-1964; fax, 202-676-0635.

International Finance Corporation (IFC)
1818 H Street, NW
Room I 9163
Washington, DC 20433
USA
Telephone: 202-477-1234 (general); 202-473-9119 (corporate relations)
Fax: 202-676-0365

The IFC is an institution within the World Bank group that provides support to the private sector in its effort to promote growth in developing countries. It actually invests in commercial enterprises. If interested, companies should contact the corporate relations unit to make proposals or obtain information.

Multilateral Investment Guarantee Agency (MIGA)
1818 H Street, NW
Washington, DC 20433
USA
Telephone: 202-473-6168
Fax: 202-477-9886

The MIGA provides guarantees against loss from noncommercial risks in foreign investment.

International Monetary Fund (IMF)
700 Nineteenth Street, NW
Washington, DC 20431
USA
Telephone: 202-623-7000

Depending on how much you want to know about the financial stability and performance of countries and their economies, you may want to explore the many publications of the International Monetary Fund. In particular, the monthly magazine accompanied by an annual yearbook, *Information Financial Statistics*, contains a wealth of economic data difficult to come by elsewhere.

Inter-American Development Bank (IDB)
1300 New York Avenue, NW
Washington, DC 20577
USA
Telephone: 202-623-1000 (general); 202-623-6278 (external relations)

The IDB was established in 1959 and focuses on economic and social development in Latin America and the Caribbean. The IDB supplements private funds as needed to support development in the borrowing member countries. As with the World Bank and IMF, it may provide technical advice to the government of the countries in which it is working. Projects are all over the lot and include sewage treatment, road construction, support for entrepreneurs, education and training, farming and fishing, and so on.

African Development Bank Headquarters
01 BP 1387
Abidjan 01
Côte d'Ivoire
Telephone: 225-20-4444
Fax: 225-21-7753

The African Development Bank seeks to aid the development of African member nations by financing projects and promoting private investment in Africa. Related to the bank is the African Development Fund, which provides financing to the poorer countries of Africa at especially low rates.

Asian Development Bank
P.O. Box 780
1099 Manila, Philippines
Street address:
6 ADB Avenue, Mandaluyong
Metro Manila, Philippines
Telephone: 63-2-711
Fax: 63-2-741-7961

With the past progress in several Asian countries, the Asian Development Bank is planning to focus its resources on specific needy nations in the area. The bank mostly finances and supports infrastructure projects.

European Bank for Reconstruction and Development
One Exchanges Square
London EC2A 2EH
England
Telephone: 44-71-338-6000
Fax: 44-71-338-6100

The European Bank for Reconstruction and Development was established in 1991 to aid in the development and transition of the countries of Central and Eastern Europe and the former Soviet Union. The bank seeks to promote private initiative. It can make loans to private enterprise, invest in equity capital, and confirm guarantees.

European Investment Bank
100 Bd Konrad Adenauer
L-2950 Luxembourg
Telephone 4379-1
Fax: 43 77 04

The mission of the European Investment Bank is to further the objectives of the European Union by making long-term financing available for sound investments. Financing is often provided in the form of individual loans and global loans to assist with development in Africa, Latin America and the Caribbean, Eastern and Central Europe, Asia, and the Mediterranean.

The European Development Fund
European Commission
Directorate General for Development
"General Financial Affairs; Relations with European Investment Bank"
Rue de la Loi, 200
B-1040 Brussels
Telephone: 32-2-295-19-08
Fax: 32-2-296-98-42

The European Development Fund is the main financing instrument of the Lome Convention and provides grants for aid programs for the 70 African, Caribbean, and Pacific countries that are signatories to this agreement with the European Union.

PHARE
European Commission, Information Unit
Directorate General External Relations
Europe and the New Independent States MO 34 3/80
Westraat 200 Rue de la Loi
B-1049 Brussels
Telephone: 32-2-299-16-00/299-14-44
Fax: 32-2-299-17-77
E-mail: phare.info@dgla.cec.be
Web Site: <www.cec.lu/en/comm/dgla/phare.html>

The Phare Programme is a European Union initiative that supports the development of a larger democratic family of nations within a prosperous and stable Europe. Phare provides know-how from a wide range of noncommercial public and private organizations to its partner countries. It acts as a multiplier by stimulating investment and responding to needs that cannot be met by others. Phare can unlock funds for important projects from other donors through studies, capital grants, guarantee schemes, and credit lines.

TACIS
European Commission
Tacis Information Office
Directorate General for External Political Relations
AN 88 1/06
Westraat 200 Rue de la Loi
B-1049 Brussels
Belgium
Telephone: 32-2-295-25-85/296-60-65
Fax: 32-2-231-04-41

The Tacis Programme is a European Union initiative to help the Newly Independent States move away from centrally planned to market economies. It provides support in the form of grant finance to foster exchange and knowledge and expertise through partnerships, links, and networks.

APPENDIX C

EUROPEAN OFFICES OF TRADE AND INDUSTRY

This list of European government Web sites provides a starting point for those wishing to locate and explore citizen-oriented information disseminated by European governments.

Austria
http://gov.austria - info.at/ForeignAffairs

Belgium
www.online.be/belgium

Denmark
www.SDN.DK/

Finland
www.vn.fi/

France
www.france.diplomatie.fr/

Germany
www.auswaertiges-amt.government.de/

Germany (Bavaria)
www.bayern.de/

Greece
web.ariadne-t.gr/

Ireland
www.ir/gov.ie

Italy
www.aipa.it/

Luxembourg
www.restena.lv/gover/

Netherlands
http://145.10.251.249/

Portugal
http://infocid.sma.pt/

Spain
www.la-moncloa.es/

Sweden
www.sb.gov.se/

United Kingdom
www.open.gov.UK/

Austria

Ministry of Economics
Stubenrint 1
1010 Vienna

Belgium

Belgium Foreign Trade Office
Emile Jacqmainlaan 162-box 36
B-1210 Brussels
Telephone: 32-2-219-44-50
Fax: 32-2-217-61-23

Flemish Foreign Trade Board
Koningsstraat 80
B-1000 Brussels
Telephone: 32-2-504-87-11
Fax: 32-2-504-88-99

Belgium Nationale Delcrederedienst (Export Insurance)
Square de Meeus 40
1040 Brussels
Belgium
Telephone: 01132-2-509-42-11
Fax: 01132-2-513-50-59

France

Department of Trade & Commerce
Yves Galland
139 Rue de Bercy
75572 Paris, Cedex 12
France
Telephone: 140-04-04-04

Germany

Ministry of Economic Affairs
Villemombler Stra 76
53123 Bonn
Germany
Telephone: 49-228-6150

Greece

Ministry of Trade
Kanigos Square
Athens, Greece
Telephone: 301-361-6241
Fax: 301-384-2642

Iceland

Ministry of Trade
Arnarhavali
150 Reykjavik
Iceland
Telephone: 354-560-9070

Ireland

Department of Tourism and Trade
Kildare Street
Dublin 2
Telephone: 353-1-662-1444
Fax: 353-1-676-6154
Web site: <www.irlgov.ie/dtt>

Italy

Ministero Del Commercio
Viale America 341
001 44 Rome Itaay
Telephone: 39-6-599-31
Fax: 39-6-59-647-494

Luxembourg

Minister of the Economy
19 Boulevard Royale
2914 Luxembourg
Grand Duchy of Luxembourg
Telephone: 352-4781

Norway

Ministry of Trade and Commerce
P.O. Box 8148 DEP
0033 Oslo, Norway
Telephone: 47-22-24-9090

Sweden

Ministry of Trade and Commerce
1033 Stockholm
Sweden
Telephone: 84052131

United Kingdom

Department of Trade and Industry
Ashdown House
123 Victoria Street
London SW1E 6RB
Telephone: 441-215-5000

Welsh Office of Overseas Trade Services
The Welsh Office
Cathays Park
Cardiff CF1 3NQ
Telephone: 01222-823547
Fax: 01222-823964
E-mail: exports@welsh-ofce.gov.uk

Other Helpful Internet Sites

Export and International Trade

http://lib.lsu.edu/bus/marketin.html
http://ciber.bus.msu.edu/busres.htm
www.dis.strath.ac.uk/business/index.html
www.isomeric.com/islink.html

Country Information

www.tradeport.org/ts/countries
www.odci.gov/cia
http://strategis.ic.gc.ca
www.embassy.org
http://lcweb.loc.gov

Addresses of Foreign Companies

www.globalyp.com
http://s17.bigyellow.com
www.europages.com
www.i-trade.com/exhibit/search

ENDNOTES

Chapter 2. Global Culture

1. Robert H. Rosen, *Global Literacies* (New York: Simon & Schuster, 1999).

2. *Ibid.*

3. Christopher Bartlett and Sumantra Ghoshal, "Going Global: Lessons from Late Movers," *Harvard Business Review* (March–April 2000): 134.

4. *Ibid.*, 135.

5. Anil Gupta and Vijay Govindarajan, "Managing Global Expansion," *Business Horizons* (March–April 2000): 52.

6. Bartlett and Ghoshal, 142.

7. SE GC Equity Team Synthesis, "Clyde Bowers plc.," (Fall 1999).

8. SE GC Enquiry Team, "Quadstone Limited," (Fall 1999).

9. Bartlett and Ghoshal, 138.

10. Niraj Dawar and Tony Frost, "Competing with Giants," *Harvard Business Review* (March–April 1999): 126.

Chapter 3. Global Marketing

1. "P&G Reorganizes To Become A Truly Global Company," *Chain Drug Review* (May 1998).

2. Ruth E. Thaler-Carter, "Whither Global Leaders," *HR Magazine* (1 May 2000).

3. Hal B. Gregersen, Allen J. Morrison, and J. Stewart Black, "Developing Leaders for the Global Frontier," *Sloan Management Review* (Fall 1998).

4. Anil Gupta and Vijay Govindarajan, "Managing Global Expansion," *Business Horizons* (March–April 2000): 50.

5. Henry Conn and George Yip, "Global Transfer of Capabilities," *Business Horizons* (January–February 1997): 23.

6. J. Jennings and L. Haughton, "It's not the BIG that eat the small . . . it's the FAST that eats the slow," *Harper Business:* (2001).

7. Christopher Bartlett and Sumantra Ghoshal, "Going Global: Lessons from Late Movers," *Harvard Business Review* (March–April 2000): 139.

8. *Ibid.*

Chapter 4. Global Account Management

1. Hui Yuk-Min, "Cooperation Form Focal Point of Global Vision," *South China Morning Post* (26 January 2001).

2. *Ibid.*

3. "Changing Sales and Business Processes Critical To Being A Global Player," press release issued by Ballard & King Communications for SPL (6 April 1999).

4. *Ibid.*

5. *Ibid.*

6. *Ibid.*

7. Jeffrey E. Garten, "The Mind of the C.E.O.," (Basic Books/ Perseus Publishing, 2001).

8. Study conducted on Global Account Management Program Success and Failure Profiles, Andrew-Ward International, Inc., 2001.

Chapter 6. Global E-business

1. "Nestlé: An Elephant Dances," *Business Week Magazine,* Int. Ed. (11 December 2000).

INDEX

ABOUT THE AUTHORS

John A. Caslione is president and CEO of Andrew-Ward International, Inc. (AWI), an international marketing and sales firm based in Chicago that specializes in assisting companies in the development and implementation of global marketing, sales, and distribution alliance strategies.

Caslione is a leading international speaker and author on global business and in the development of strategic supplier alliances.

As the key principal at AWI, Caslione has assisted companies in developing global business strategies in more than 70 countries including the United States, Canada, South America, Europe (Western, Central, and Eastern), Russia and the CIS, the Middle East, Asia, China, India, and Africa.

Caslione is also a member of the faculty of Southern Methodist University's (SMU) Executive Development Program in its Edwin L. Cox School of Business in Dallas, where he leads key executive management programs he has developed in global business development and distribution.

Caslione earned his MBA from the University of New York and his Doctorate of Law (JD) from Illinois Institute of Technology's Chicago-Kent College of Law.

Caslione resides in Lake Forest, Illinois, with Andrea, his wife, and their two children, Allison and Christopher.

John A. Caslione
President and CEO
Andrew-Ward International, Inc.
222 Wisconsin Avenue, Suite 102
Lake Forest, IL 60045
Telephone: 847-615-5450
FAX: 847-615-5451
E-mail: *john@caslione.com*
Web site: <www.caslione.com>

Andrew R. Thomas is an accomplished journalist, author, and global business expert. As an investigative journalist, he has covered global political and economic issues for a number of publications in North and South America and has conducted business and traveled to more than 100 countries on all seven continents.

Thomas is the author of the bestselling book, *Air Rage: Crisis in the Skies,* and host of the Web site AirRage.org. He is also the coauthor of the benchmark book *The Power of Female Entrepreneurship: A Global Argument.*

Thomas has served on the faculties of the University of Akron, the University of Toledo, and La Universidad de Guayaquil in Ecuador. He holds graduate degrees in international relations and Latin America studies.

He lives in the Cleveland area with his wife, Jacqueline, and their two children, Paul Bryan and Alana Regina.

Andrew R. Thomas
6538 Cross Creek Trail
Brecksville, OH 44141
Telephone: 440-546-0821
Fax: 440-546-0568
E-mail: *arthomas29@aol.com*
Web site: <www.AirRage.org>